chaos
to
calm

praise for the essentialists

'An inspiring 'how-to' guide for how to find calm confidence
within yourself, which is so important for helping you live
your best life, every day.'

kristina karlsson

Founder, Kikki. K

'The ultimate recipe to help you to find the courage to be
the most important person in your life and guide you towards
great acceptance and happiness.'

deborah hutton

Founder, Balance by Deborah Hutton

'Lyndall and Shannah, both experts in their fields, motivate
individuals to evaluate how they currently handle multiple demands
in an ever-changing environment, and to consider new strategies
for managing stress, personally and professionally. This set
of foundational life skills helps to maintain focus and
direction in our professional and personal life.'

paul fog

General Manager, Wealth Division NAB

'People managers need life skills so they can successfully
mentor and motivate others to take charge of their lives.
This is the perfect handbook for every leader.'

colleen callander

CEO, Sportsgirl

chaos
to
calm

take
control
with
confidence

Shannah Kennedy & Lyndall Mitchell

VIKING
an imprint of
PENGUIN BOOKS

contents

dedication

Michael, Jack and Mia. We are team Kennedy, our unit rocks.

Ever-grateful for what we have each and every day.

May we forever as a family practise these skills.

shannah

Scott, Poppy and Grace, I love you to the moon and
back a million times over.

Thanks Mum, for always encouraging me to stand tall.

And Dad, for being my rock.

lyndall

foreword

a personal uprising: that is what *Chaos to Calm* offers us. The rapid pace of life today can often make you feel like you don't have time to actually live. This book is a powerful tool designed to support you as you exit the 'stress express' and curate the life you want – one that will serve your heart, mind and body. It will show you a path paved with passion and purpose – the path from chaos to calm.

We are living in a time where many of us are feeling too tired to keep running, yet don't have the confidence to stop. We need an intervention – a time-out to re-awaken and reclaim our better selves. If we could simply give ourselves permission to catch our breath and reconnect with our true selves, we could carefully realign, reinvent and remember what is really important to us. You have begun your time out with this book.

Lyndall and Shannah's expertise in the science of living well is renowned. They are courageous enough to question the unsustainable pace of life and the limiting beliefs that we have adopted about our personal possibilities. They demand we rebel against modern trends toward self-oppression and the mass movement toward mediocrity. As Gandhi said, 'there is more to life than increasing its speed'.

Upon finishing *Chaos to Calm* I felt inspired to rise up and become the best possible version of myself. I feel confident that you, too, will feel the courage, confidence and conviction to live up to your best self and follow your own path from chaos to calm.

dr james rouse

Confidence

What a word.
What a feeling.
What a necessity.

Self-confidence is a skill
that can be learned.
Work on developing
your confidence and
watch your life improve
day by day.

feeling tired, stressed, too busy and out of control? Are you overscheduled, overwhelmed and in need of some rest and relaxation? This book is designed to help you take action in essential areas of your life that will help you gain control. The topics will educate, inspire and show you how to build resilience and confidence in this fast-paced, time-poor, over-scheduled world.

Confidence is the key to really living your life on your own terms, with calmness, clarity, meaning and inner harmony. Healthy confidence is a vital ingredient for personal success and happiness. When we have it, we feel good about ourselves; we are calm, assured, have a healthy sense of control and everything seems possible. 'Have confidence!' is one of the most essential pieces of advice you'll receive in life – but it's no help at all if you don't know how. How often do you hear people say, 'I don't have the confidence to do that'? You know what confident people look and act like, the advantages that come their way, how calmly they go through life and that they have something worth emulating. How do you get there, though?

This book offers a simple step-by-step approach to real things you can do, by yourself, to regain your naturally confident, balanced and motivated self. We combine theory and practice with a fresh approach that is founded on scientific research and have included practical ideas, techniques and strategies for your personal success.

introduction

It's here to assist you to refuel – your pitstop when you need to have a quick refresh on how to improve your self-esteem and believe in yourself again. Every day is a new day in which you have the choice to take back your personal power, and these pages are jam-packed with advice and skills that you can put into practice straight away.

As life coaches with a combined thirty years of experience, we've found that a lack of confidence is usually the number one issue behind everything our clients need to address. Our clients are successful professionals who want to improve their precious lives. They've achieved a great deal, but are still privately troubled about whether they're 'good enough'. Most do not know how to build confidence and wellness, or what steps they need to take to start building a more solid belief in themselves. These are the life skills we teach: we help you start knowing yourself and building strong skills to love who are you personally and professionally.

It is becoming apparent that more needs to be done to help people overcome low self-esteem, because it can have devastating effects. Developing the life skills to support confidence is something we are very passionate about, and we teach and practise it daily.

what is confidence, anyway?

Confidence is about being able to make the right choice for you; it is an overarching attitude and the basis of self-belief and worth. It is about assuring your interior self that your exterior self has value. Confidence is the characteristic that distinguishes those who do from those who

chaos to calm

simply imagine. It is based on life skills that keep us connected to our authentic selves, and when it is built with these skills, it will help the subconscious mind start to trust itself. Sometimes people confuse confidence with arrogance, but it only takes a minute to understand the difference between the two. An arrogant person is someone who feels they are superior, who is lost in their own self-importance and who proceeds through life with a sense of entitlement. By contrast, a confident person trusts their own judgement but also has a strong enough sense of self-worth to know when they should ask for advice or accept help.

what does a lack of confidence look like?

Many of us have had confidence-robbers in our lives; sometimes these influences will destroy your confidence on purpose and sometimes it's unintentional. Teachers, parents, peer groups, partners, social media, movies and much more can influence how we feel about ourselves, sometimes to our detriment. Research tells us our confidence levels are wired in during childhood, but the good news is that we can rewire ourselves and change the situation. So it is time to connect back with yourself, protect the asset that is you and create your own way to plug the holes and fill your confidence tank.

Dr Joe Rubino, author of *The Self-Esteem Book*, states that 85 per cent of the world's population are affected by low self-esteem. People depend excessively on the approval of others in order to feel great about themselves.

> A person without confidence is like a jumbo jet sitting on the tarmac with an empty tank, no captain, passengers or flight plan.

These people suffer from a fear of failure, avoid growth and joy in their lives and don't take risks. In contrast to this, a person with healthy, balanced confidence can take a compliment but is also willing to risk the disapproval of others occasionally because they trust their own abilities and will protect what is most important to them for happiness.

Lack of confidence leads us to be needy and try to fit in to impress others and gain acceptance. The danger here is that we are not being true to ourselves; rather than the drivers of our own lives, we are passengers unable to sleep well at night knowing we have made the best choices. Succumbing to peer group pressure, substance abuse, getting into dangerous situations, feeling lonely in a crowd, doing things because others want you to regardless of your own feelings, trying to impress others with the things you own, only living on the surface and being reactionary are some of the results of a lack of self-confidence and self-knowledge. Self-sabotage comes from not having a good skill set and having no solid foundations on which to make decisions.

Our desire to fit in, to be connected, is a result of our new style of living where life is fast. We are time-poor and our human-to-human communication skills are decreasing due to technology and the way we communicate via social media. Online bullying can leave a person feeling that there's nowhere to hide, and the information overload telling you to be better, skinnier, healthier, fitter and richer can contribute to low self-esteem. The highly edited profiles we see on social media mean we are often comparing our real lives with the pretend lives of others, which can contribute to feelings of inferiority.

By contrast, if we were comfortable in our own skin and could really look in the mirror, accept and love who we are and have a great vision and skill set for our own journey and best life, we would feel a real sense of confidence and trust in ourselves to make great decisions.

Learning the skill set to support our own confidence will open us up to following our own desires and help us reject the distractions that cause chaos in our lives – the ones that create time famines and disconnect us from ourselves and others.

why do we need life skills for confidence?

The really important life skills are not taught at school. They are the most important skills to learn, and often we discover them too late. Every human being needs to feel loved and connected to others, and to have a healthy sense of self-confidence to navigate through life and trust themselves. You must know yourself, love yourself and own your sense of achievement and inner harmony. Your internal compass will help you make great choices as you gain full awareness and ownership of yourself.

Taking time out for self-reflection is the most critical, and yet most underrated, personal happiness tool. Self-reflection builds confidence as you consciously identify what is working well and what is not. In order to fuel new self-confidence you need to learn and adopt new behaviours that feed your perception of self and allow you to flourish and evolve.

So many times we have heard the phrase, 'If we had the confidence to do it we would.' And, 'I am not sure I can do that.' Do you feel you lack the confidence to have a go? To speak your mind? To make a good decision for yourself? To stick to a goal and succeed? To be vulnerable and connected to other people? To unlock the door to a pathway to where you would love to be? In this book, we give you the skills to turn all these thoughts around.

knowing yourself + developing skills to support yourself
= confidence

We teach our clients to think of their level of confidence as a tank that needs filling quite often if it is to be resilient, strong and reliable. We have identified sixteen essential life skills that keep the tank full so you can make decisions with clarity, live confidently in your skin, have choices and, most importantly, can look in the mirror and love the person you see looking back at you.

what are we striving for?

Gaining a great store of healthy confidence-building skills and practices gives you back your personal power, allows you to start dissolving any conflict around you and helps you to make sound decisions for yourself. It enables you to have great conversations and feel good about yourself, and allows you the space for reflection you need to change and renew your habits so they keep working for you.

Owning your confidence means that you are totally at peace with yourself in every moment, experience and interaction. You don't make apologies for feeling nervous, being softly spoken, introverted or loud. You are just you.

confidence tank
self check

	agree	disagree
I am optimistic and generally positive.		
I make good decisions.		
It's okay to be angry.		
I believe in myself.		
I trust my intuition.		
The world is a beautiful place.		
It's okay for me to make mistakes.		
I love and value myself.		
I can allow myself to feel sad.		
I believe that I can change.		
I can forgive myself.		
I can say 'no' when I need to.		
I express my feelings easily.		
I deserve the best that life has to offer.		

How did you answer these questions? Are you feeling powerful, confident, decisive and at one with the world, or are you feeling threatened, insecure and out of control? In other words, are you feeling high or low in self-confidence?

Listed below are some of the things that over the years our clients have associated with having low or high self-confidence.

high self-confidence	low self-confidence
Feeling peaceful and calm	Feeling overwhelmed and stressed
Feeling secure	Feeling insecure
A sense of enthusiasm and vitality	Lethargy and lack of motivation
Having realistic expectations	Having unrealistic expectations
Feeling in control	Feeling out of control
Work and life are in balance	Feeling burned out and overworked
Feeling connected	Feeling isolated
Having self-respect	Having no self-respect
Feeling authentic	Feeling like a fraud
Enthusiasm	Depression
A sense of success	A sense of failure
Feeling 'in the flow'	Feeling stuck
Strong personal boundaries	Poor personal boundaries
A sense of dignity	A sense of shame
Quality relationships	Draining relationships
Being able to communicate clearly	Muddled communication
Making empowered decisions	Making guilty, burdened decisions

Add your own here:

high self-confidence	low self-confidence

what does confident behaviour look like?

Your level of confidence can show in many ways: how you speak, what you say, your body language, your behaviour and your own self-talk. Look at the following comparisons of common confident behaviours versus behaviours seen in people with low self-confidence. Take a moment to see which thoughts or actions you are familiar with in yourself and the people close to you.

confident behaviour	behaviour associated with low self-confidence
Trusting your own decisions	Relying solely on other people's opinions
Showing a willingness to take risks	Avoiding risks and staying in your comfort zone because you fear failure
An ability to admit to mistakes, learn from them and move on	Trying to cover up mistakes
Not needing to brag about your accomplishments	Needing to boast
Being able to accept compliments with grace	Refusing to accept compliments

As you can see from these examples, low self-confidence can be destructive, and it often manifests itself as negativity. Confident people are generally more positive – they believe in themselves and their abilities, and they also believe in living life to the full.

the journey ahead

Even the most confident people have days of low self-confidence. We are human beings, not machines. This book was written as your handbook for life, a wellness tapas menu for you to pick up any time and refamiliarise yourself with a valuable skill to master. Each chapter starts with a general explanation of the topic it will focus on, then moves on to examples and exercises you can do, then provides a list of 'power thoughts' to help you, a summary, and some inspirational quotes. Remember, practice is the key to mastering any skill: just like riding a bike, you will retain most skills forever if you just keep having a go.

This book will be a valuable resource for you as you start moving from chaos to calm. We wish you an amazing experience as you unlock each chapter and enable yourself to grow, evolve, flourish and live each day with confidence.

Confidence is a mindset. Confidence is a decision. You have to decide to be and feel confident and drive your life from there.

mirror, mirror on the wall

---

get to know yourself

An essential part of
building confidence is
getting to know yourself.
So many of us know
what we don't want,
and how we don't want
to be and look, but how
many know what we do
want? When you look in the
mirror, do you see a person
truly and authentically
committed to the path
of your future goals,
success and values?

We are all made up of many layers, like a perfectly formed onion. Getting to know yourself is getting to know the layers that form you. Peeling back the layers is essential in getting to know yourself in a much deeper and more meaningful way. Really seeing yourself is a vital step to loving who you are.

Part of this process is connecting with yourself again and finding out what you really want to be doing on your own unique path. This is your responsibility to manage and is something that can't be done for you by others.

You can work on getting to know yourself by doing the seemingly simple exercise of looking into the mirror with a purpose every morning. That purpose is to get to know yourself even better than you do right now. To connect to a part of yourself that knows what you are here for, knows how to live authentically, and listens to your deepest inner desires. One of our clients went to a finishing school, hoping for some great life tips, and the first thing they told her was that she should lose a little weight. She was perfectly healthy, fit and happy, and this advice threw her into a spin. However, she listened to her inner self and realised she was happy with who she was, and decided not to go back.

We do this exercise first with almost all our clients, even those with great confidence: it's so important to know and love who you are. So often our clients feel that someone else is in control of their lives.

mirror, mirror on the wall

Deep inner confidence comes with taking control, building a deep connection to yourself and loving who you are. Building a strong relationship with the person in the mirror allows you to make the decisions that work best for you. As everyone looks different, feels different and has different life experiences, it is time to be less influenced by others and to start a great and healthy relationship with the person who is there with you for life: your own best counsel and friend, yourself.

'Who am I?' It is one thing to think about this question in passing; quite another to actually look into your own eyes and seriously give it some thought. So often we spend too much time on the treadmill of life without clarity about our future or who we want to be. This question may raise a collection of different thoughts and beliefs that you have developed over your lifetime.

You were born with confidence. When you witness a child in front of the mirror you can clearly see how connected they are to themselves. They are not judgemental, worrying about their hair, the size of their nose and all the other small things adults criticise in themselves. In their minds they are totally loveable. They are free.

Then, life happens. Insecurities can develop when people say things to us; we are influenced by parents, teachers, peers, media – the list goes on. Our insecurities come out. 'I am not good enough, smart or successful enough, beautiful or strong enough, not interesting, thin or rich enough.' Sound familiar? Self-judgement, a negative commentary running beneath the surface of our minds, is just a habit that needs rewiring. When you do this, you can establish a friendship with yourself again, allowing you to reconnect and build on owning your thoughts and bringing confidence back into your life. It doesn't cost money, and the good news is it doesn't take much effort to look in the mirror.

When we continually judge ourselves we are always looking for the worst, due to the brain's negativity bias. Studies have shown that our brains are simply more likely to notice and retain bad news. Add in glamorous magazines, our obsession with selfies, heavily edited pictures, celebrities and other examples of seeming perfection and we can soon see why we tend to judge and highlight the negative parts of ourselves when we look in the mirror.

The purpose of mirror work is to stop judging yourself and to start seeing and connecting with who you are. This is the first action we ask all of our clients to take, no matter who they are or how successful they are; all the answers are in the mirror. This is a skill to use forever to help build a foundation of confidence, self-esteem and self-worth.

Stop judging yourself and start seeing and connecting with who you are. A strong foundation of confidence and self-worth will help you to make the choices that are best for you.

benefits
of mirror
work

Getting to know yourself
and seeing your essence

Establishing a deeper connection
with yourself

Finding your authentic purpose in life

Opening the way to listen to
your own inner desires

Rewiring your mind into believing in,
loving and approving of yourself

each time we look in the mirror we are confronted with ourselves; if we want others to be kind to us, we need to start by being kind to ourselves. Each day is a new beginning, allowing us to reset, refocus and refresh. You will notice there are mirrors everywhere: in the bathroom, in the car, in lounge rooms, bedrooms, shops, offices and cafes. You can say hello, give yourself approval and work on your confident self all day long.

A client once said that he looked in the mirror and could not see anything other than his outer shell. We suggested he try the exercise at least five times per day. After a week still he looked in the mirror and felt totally disconnected from himself. After two weeks he called and said he had started to make friends with the man in the mirror; he'd started to acknowledge his presence and opened up a positive dialogue. His posture began to change, he started being kinder to himself and his family, and he replaced the negative thoughts that came up with positives, taking opportunities to work on recurring troubling thoughts. He even noticed his reflection in the glass oven door one day. He went from being a man who didn't care about himself much, who had no self-esteem or confidence, who didn't know who he was at all, to being a man of beautiful deep inner harmony and assurance, a man who owned his life and thoughts as best he could. He started to flourish in life again.

Mirror work is about starting to feel comfortable in your own skin. Truly looking into the mirror can help you build a truly connected relationship with yourself. Looking into the mirror dissolves fears and worries and replaces them with self-confidence and calm. Remember, this is a skill to build on every day. A skill set to support yourself and stay connected to yourself for life.

mirror, mirror on the wall

the mirror technique

exercise to love and approve of yourself

This may initially seem silly, or you might be worried about what people think. Notice your judgements and resistance to the new and unfamiliar, and don't let them get in the way.

You can do this at home every morning and then reinforce it at every opportunity throughout the day: any time you pass a mirror, say something positive to yourself. Be your own cheerleader, take yourself lightly and have some fun with whatever it is that is really challenging you.

The more often you reinforce the positive, the faster you'll be able to reprogram your mind and your confidence tank will start to fill.

'Love is a mirror:
it reflects only
your essence,
if you have
the courage to
look in its face.'

---

rumi

how to

Start by doing this exercise for one minute first thing when you wake up and again before you go to bed. Gradually build up to five minutes.

Stand in front of a mirror.

Acknowledge yourself and look into your eyes.

Find one thing you like about yourself.

Tell yourself what you'd like to hear.

Tell your body how grateful you are for how it supports you.

Pick something specific to appreciate and
tell your body how much you love it.

Ask yourself, 'What can I do to make you happy today?'

Ask yourself, 'What is the best decision I can make today?'

Affirm that you are calm and confident.

Say to yourself that you are empowered today
and making choices that fill your tank.

Make peace with the person in the mirror:
you are your most important project.

Here's why the mirror technique is the best confidence-building exercise:

- You'll start feeling more comfortable in your own skin.
- You'll accept the way you look and behave.
- Your communication skills will improve as you get better at communicating with yourself.
- Each time you do the exercise, you'll give yourself a self-esteem and motivation boost.
- You'll be more positive.
- You'll start believing in your own abilities and thus be ready to try new stuff.
- You won't feel inferior to others any more.
- You'll appreciate yourself for who you are and will embrace your good qualities.
- You won't be afraid to look people in the eyes.
- You'll appear more confident in front of others.
- You'll have a higher opinion of yourself.
- You won't have so many doubts.
- You'll be more decisive.
- You'll set higher goals and will feel more confident of your chances of reaching them.
- You'll look and be stronger and people will start treating you differently.

summary

- The mirror technique is a confidence-building exercise.

- Connecting with yourself, accepting yourself and loving yourself are the primary purposes of mirror work.

- Use the mirror exercise as the start of building your confidence to support yourself in life.

- Using the mirror technique daily will enable you to make the best possible decisions for yourself and will help you to find inner calm.

- Notice that there are mirrors everywhere that you can use to connect with yourself every day.

- The more you accept, love and appreciate yourself, the more confidence you will cultivate.

- It is not someone else's job to fill your tank; it's up to you to keep your tank full.

power thoughts

I'm proud of myself.
_____

I love and approve of who I am.
_____

I am calm and relaxed.
_____

I believe in myself.
_____

I'm self-reliant.
_____

I feel confident about my life plans.
_____

I have the potential to do great things with my life.
_____

Others respect me.
_____

I deserve the best and only good things are coming my way.
_____

trains
of thought

own your mindset

Starting to own
your thoughts and
reactions to situations
and building a pathway
for inner strength
and confidence are
simple skills that,
when practised regularly,
can change your world.
The power to control
our thoughts is the key
to a better life.

for years, it was thought that the brain's capabilities were fixed and that we were stuck with what we were born with. We now know that our thoughts can govern our words, behaviours and actions, accelerating stress, ageing and illness. In recent years, research has discovered that you can actually create new pathways in the brain, and with effort, train it to behave differently. The brain has the ability to not only change, adapt and learn, but also to actually rewire itself, so changing our thoughts is not only possible, it is achievable for everyone.

Did you know that on average we produce as many as 50000 thoughts per day, according to the USA's National Science Foundation? That means our minds are incredibly active. It's important to note, though, that up to 98 per cent of these thoughts are the same ones you had yesterday, the day before and the day before that.

Unfortunately, most of us are wired in such a way that up to 80 per cent of our thoughts are negative. For many people, negative thinking is so normal that it is as natural as breathing. When the running commentary in your mind is negatively influenced, you will beat yourself up for every perceived mistake, criticising yourself for not measuring up to the all-singing, all-dancing vision of perfection that your internal judge thinks you should adhere to. So often, thinking about our feelings and abilities, judging ourselves and making ourselves the stars of our own melodrama tends to limit and inhibit us.

trains of thought

For a moment, imagine those 50000 thoughts as trains. Imagine standing at a busy railway station where there are 50000 trains coming through. That is an incredibly busy station, isn't it? So often we can get on the trains of self-doubt, worry or frustration; we can be on these trains of thought and not even realise. This is what we call being on autopilot, and these thoughts are more distracting than they are helpful. They can lead us to procrastinate, waste time and get sidetracked from our goals and our purpose.

Once you start to see the 50000 trains and understand the concept of being on autopilot, you can also see that you actually have a choice as to which train you would like to board, even though it sometimes may not feel that way. Of course, no one is completely immune to getting on the wrong train – even though we've been teaching this concept for a long time, we're still vulnerable ourselves; however, we are much quicker at noticing now and getting off, as we know those trains won't get us to where we want to be.

We like to compare it to going to the gym, because training your mind is very similar to getting physically fit. When we continually pursue unhelpful thinking, we build the muscles of stress, resentment and worry. The more often we exercise it, the bigger the muscle becomes.

Training our minds takes effort and commitment, just like going to the gym. Just as you work out your biceps to get stronger, we are working the muscle of attention, focus and purpose. The more effort we expend, the better our results will be. You don't go to the gym once and think that will make you fit forever; similarly, you don't do one mind-focused activity and have positive, calm and confident thoughts forever. This is a cumulative practice that takes time and effort.

chaos to calm

'Mind is
everything;
we become
what we think.'

———————————

buddha

One of our favourite books is *Mindset: The New Psychology of Success* by the Stanford University psychologist Carol Dweck. Dweck researched the concept that most people have one of two mindsets: either a fixed or a growth mindset. Having a growth mindset means you believe that your skills and intelligence are things that can be developed and improved. Having a fixed mindset means you believe that your skills and intelligence are set and can't be changed. Her research showed that the growth mindset is what fosters grit, determination and a strong work ethic within people of all ages. The research also indicated that people within a growth mindset learn, grow and achieve more, and are happier than people who have fixed mindsets. Now that's a great train of thought to get on board!

The table opposite outlines the key characteristics (or symptoms) of the two mindsets. See which one you relate to.

When you foster your growth mindset, you'll discover that all your abilities can be developed through dedication and hard work – brains and talent are just the starting point. Knowing this helps to create the love of learning and the resilience that together are essential for great achievement. Virtually everyone who is outstanding in their field has these qualities.

Another way to look at it is to imagine that these neural pathways are like walking tracks in the bush. Some of these walking tracks are more well-worn than others.

For some of us, the walking track of resentment may be well worn, or the track of self-berating, or perhaps the belief that we can't change.

Start training! The mind is a muscle that needs to be exercised.

	fixed mindset		growth mindset
	People with this mindset tend to:		People with this mindset tend to:
	be easily defeated		be persistent
	respond badly to criticism		learn from feedback
	feel threatened by the talents of others		be inspired by the success of others
	dislike change		love a challenge
	think effort is unnecessary		have a strong work ethic

this can lead to under-perfomance and an unwillingness to learn new things

this leads to high achievement and confidence

One of our clients, Jack, spent so many years on the track of frustration and negativity that it resulted in a very fixed mindset. He constantly felt overwhelmed and unhappy with any result that was less than perfect. We showed him how to understand the patterns that were governing his thoughts, and he slowly started building his growth mindset, developing the ability to focus on effort rather than results. He found himself feeling much calmer and less stressed, eventually finding that he was actually in control of his thoughts. We identified what Jack wanted to achieve and helped him create some future pathways for the thoughts that were actually positive and exciting. Once this process had started, it built its own momentum and began to outweigh the negative, and Jack was able to create a future he felt inspired by. Now he looks back on that time and can't believe how far he has come, simply by working on his ability to adapt, learn and grow.

To take you from resentment and worry to gratitude and grace, we need to create some new walking paths. This is like cutting a new walkway in the bush. The first time you do this, it is going to be hard to break through and you will probably meet with resistance. The second time you take the path, it will feel a little more familiar, and the third time it will feel more familiar still, and you may even be able to enjoy the surroundings and the view. As you continue, you're building the automatic ability for your brain to travel this pathway.

The other pathways and old habits are still going to be there; we cannot erase them, unfortunately. What we can do is focus on building the track for the new path so it becomes more well-worn, and the old paths are no longer needed. When you think of any of the old pathways that didn't serve you well, or the old, clunky train, your objective is to see their signs and be able to choose an alternative route. The ability to choose your path involves learning to be conscious of how you react, and how to feel less alienated from your thought process. This takes practice; it's not a matter of trying to stop your thoughts or fight with them, but of learning not to get on board any old train of thought that comes into your mind, or just walk the same well-worn track. Any time you find yourself on a train that is going to govern rather than guide you, you'll know that you can simply get off again at the next stop.

Reflect on your day yesterday and ask yourself how much time you spent on autopilot. Did your thoughts help or hinder you in getting where you want to be? If you feel you spent too much time on autopilot, then there are some ways to help steer your thoughts in the right direction and keep your train on the track you want.

By taking control of our trains of thought, we start to focus our attention in a directed way and the result is a happier, more joyful life. Sure, it requires more effort to live this way; however the benefits far outweigh the costs, in ways you may never have dreamed of. This is such a central part of confidence. If you can, think of some times when you were thriving, when you felt unstoppable and on top of the world. What do these memories have in common? Were you feeling confident? The brain and our thoughts are the control room of our happiness.

Reflect for a moment: would you speak to your closest friend, your children or your mentor in the same way you speak to yourself? If the answer is no, then ask yourself, why is it okay to speak to myself like this? Remember, everything in your life starts with you, so why is it okay not to treat the central person in your world with the same respect you would give the closest people in your life?

trains of thought

So often clients of ours feel overwhelmed, overworked and over-scheduled, and this leads to feeling worried and stressed; it can also wear on the body over time. When we worry, we're occupied with the past or the future. When we are able to choose our thoughts, we instantly reduce our stress and are able to be more present, engaging in the relationships that really matter to us. You'll find you have more energy for the hobbies you're inspired by, the work you find purpose in, and even everyday experiences will go from seeming humdrum to engaging.

how to

First, ask yourself if the way you think is working for you and supporting you to feel confident. Are you on a train that is going to help you achieve confidence and inner self-belief? If the answer is no, here are some top tips to get your trains on the right tracks.

1. **Be playful** A serious attitude has its place, but so does lightheartedness. Studies show that children who do not have enough play interaction can grow into unmotivated adults. Luckily, we can fix this by spending some time being playful every day.

2. **Take time out from thinking** This is a little different from doing nothing. Our minds are very active: we have so much information coming in throughout the day, especially as we're constantly connected to information technology. It's easy to feel bombarded. Our minds need rest, time to wind down and top up the tank of creativity. Develop your hobbies and interests so you can have some time every week when you are absorbed in something you enjoy.

3. **Practise forgiveness** Holding a grudge is stressful, which in turn is bad for your health. Forgiveness does not mean rolling over or being a doormat. Forgiveness involves letting go of past wrongs. Forgiveness is often not a one-shot deal. Old grudges can pop up unexpectedly,

seemingly from nowhere. Conduct a 'grudge scan' to see if you are holding on to something that is squashing your happiness. Let it go – even if just for today.

4. **Practise self-compassion**   Forgive yourself. Turn the grudge scan inward. Is there something you keep beating yourself up about? Again, let it go – just for today.

5. **Practise sympathetic joy**   This is a term used by Buddhists that means taking delight in others' good fortune. Take a look around you. Observe the good fortune of others. If you struggle with jealousy (a real happiness zapper), sympathetic joy can help. Try to rejoice in the success of others rather than feeling envious. Start by focusing on the people close to you, then move to those you feel neutral about, and gradually work towards those who elicit stronger emotions.

6. **Look at how you start conversations**   Of course we sometimes need to talk about the things that aren't going well, but where possible, try to get in the habit of starting conversations positively. Make a commitment to yourself that where possible, you will begin all conversations with one positive comment, reflection or event. From here you set the pace of the conversation and encourage others to share their best moments rather than their worst. It is a subtle change and it can make a big difference to the kind of people you attract, the way you feel and your relationships.

All of these tips help to top up your confidence tank as you stay true to what's important to you and your body. Choose to feel and act confidently and ditch those destructive critical trains of thought forever. They are obsolete; they will never work for you and they have no place in a confident and happy self.

self-talk examples

negative	positive
I don't know how.	I can learn, I can do anything.
It's too hard.	There is a way, and I will find it.
I'm not smart enough.	I am smart and I can find a solution.
I'm too tired.	This is important and I can get this done now.
I've never done this before.	There is always a first time; I can learn anything.
It will never work.	It can work and I can find a way to make it.
I'll do it tomorrow.	I'll start today and get this done on time.
There's too much to do.	Let's start with the most important things and get this done one thing at a time.

summary

- We have, on average, 50000 thoughts per day and we can train our minds to be in alignment with our goals and purpose.

- A growth mindset is believing that you have the ability to develop, versus a fixed mindset where you believe you are defined by inborn traits.

- Begin your conversations with a positive comment, reflection or action.

- Find the thoughts that need to change. If you want to be more optimistic, you first need to identify where you are most negative, and work out the thought patterns that need to be changed.

- Positive thinking means that you find solutions, approach negative events differently and focus on having things work out for the best instead of always anticipating the worst. You want to aim to see the glass as half-full and not half-empty.

power
thoughts

I thrive on challenges.

I see opportunities in every situation.

I see the best in everyone around me.

I focus on my strengths and abilities.

I have the courage to try new things.

I have no fear of what others may think.

I have confidence in my abilities.

I am on the train to 'I can do this'.

shark
versus
seaweed

---

manage stress and anxiety

Have you ever felt overwhelmed by looming deadlines, or a sense of feeling generally confused, easily distracted, forgetful, worried, anxious, quick to anger, easily frustrated, despondent and depressed or prone to aimless mental wandering? These can all be traced back to feeling either a low, moderate or high level of stress.

We often use the word 'stress' to describe emotional, mental and physical effects on our bodies, such as muscle tension, headaches, insomnia, nervousness, jaw clenching and difficulty breathing. 'Stress' has become a commonly used term which covers a wide range of daily experiences. The culture of the Western workplace, and that of many other parts of the world, is predominantly fuelled by stress, sleep deprivation and burnout. It's the stress of feeling overworked, too busy, over-connected on social media and under-connected with ourselves and the people closest to us.

Managing your stress is vitally important for your health and wellbeing. Even taking just five or ten minutes per day to relieve stress will improve the quality of your life dramatically. Your quality of life will improve greatly when you know you have the skills to combat everyday stressors.

Stress is the body's natural response to a challenging situation. Our stress response has evolved to be used when we are in danger as an emergency response. Imagine yourself swimming in the ocean when you are confronted by a 6-metre pointer shark. Your body goes into its natural fight-or-flight mode to get you out of danger and safely to shore. However, what happens more regularly is we'll be having a relaxing swim in the ocean when something brushes past our leg; in a panic we'll go straight into our full stress response, then look down and realise it is just a piece of seaweed. How many times in your day do you treat normal,

shark versus seaweed

everyday events like a white pointer shark? The guy who cuts you off in traffic, a challenging work meeting, the next exam, the next business deal. We often trigger our stress response for normal, everyday events. The wear and tear on our minds and bodies this creates is not only unhealthy, it is unsustainable.

The brain actually has trouble telling the difference between a shark and seaweed, so it very diligently delivers the responses it knows, whether mild, moderate or extreme. Too often our fight-or-flight responses are being triggered day in, day out, which is not how they are most useful. When it is working correctly, our stress response will switch on only every so often, then switch off as soon as it is no longer needed.

Try thinking of your body as your personal bank account. There are activities you can consciously do that put 'deposits' in your account to keep it flourishing, just like saving up for something on your wish list. When you have a stress response, it is the same as making a withdrawal from your account. It's normal and natural to make a withdrawal every now and then, however if it's happening every day, sometimes five times a day or more, then that's going to deplete your account pretty quickly; if you let it go over time, then your account will get overdrawn. When your body gets to the point of being 'overdrawn', it will have a negative effect on your health, your happiness and ultimately your confidence.

A stressor such as a shark is a clearly identifiable trigger for your stress response; however, the stressors for your mind aren't always so obvious. Most of the time, the threat is imaginary; your mind can't tell what's real and what's not. It believes what you tell it. It trusts your judgment and follows your every command.

Once we activate our fight-or-flight response, a number of reactions take place in our bodies. The thinking part of our brain shuts down, which doesn't matter if you don't need to make decisions or be strategic, but for most of us it will be a problem. Your digestion shuts down, so even if you are going to the effort of having your morning green smoothie, your body won't be absorbing all of the vital nutrients. Your immune function also shuts down, so you might find yourself getting sick more often, and your sex drive goes out the window, which is not great for anyone!

If you can, think back to a time when you experienced a real threat. In that situation you were probably not thinking of anything else. This is a type of 'extreme mindfulness'. You were not thinking about your next holiday or what you were having for dinner. You were totally focused on what was happening in that moment, because you had to be. Often we get so anxious and worried about what might or might not happen in the future, or we relive past events so often that it doesn't matter that these events are only in our heads. If we're not mindful, we take the imaginary threat to be real and activate our stress response automatically.

Most people have had the experience of a bout of sleeplessness that's involved thinking about all the projects in their lives: 'Will I or won't I get this business deal over the line?', 'Will I make the deadline?', 'Will I or won't I get the job I'm going for?' The next day, it is easy to see there was no actual threat in your bedroom, however, at the point when you activate those thoughts, you also activate your stress response. This then makes all the anxiety-laden

Managing your stress is vitally important for your health and wellbeing.

fight-or-flight chemicals rush through your body, making it impossible to sleep. It's the kind of recurring pattern that makes us exhausted as it wears us down.

This stress response can be triggered inappropriately; some of the most common ways are listed below:

When we imagine situations to be more threatening than they really are. Have you ever had a meeting that you thought was going to be incredibly challenging and confronting, where you've prepared for every worst-case scenario, focused on the negative outcomes and imagined the situation to be far worse than is actually possible? One of us had this experience when she was younger and wanted to ask for a pay rise. She had every avenue covered as to why she should get it. She worked it over and over in her mind, anticipating a difficult conversation, then in the meeting her boss said, 'Yes, I was about to chat to you about this. I think a pay rise is well deserved.' She'd convinced herself it was going to be painful, confronting and challenging and it was exactly the opposite: a brief meeting with the result she wanted.

When we worry about events that may not actually happen. Ever found yourself dreaming up an Oscar-winning performance to cope with something far worse than will ever be possible? We certainly have, and it can feel incredibly real until you ask yourself, 'What am I thinking about this for?'

When we repeatedly go over events that have already come and gone. We all tend to be really good at giving ourselves a hard time over something we said or did, even if it happened years ago. In fact it is incredible how we can remember the details of when something went wrong versus all the other things that do go our way. Our minds look for the negative angle; this is our negativity bias, as mentioned previously. Human beings have evolved to notice and respond more forcibly to the negative, since doing so helped our ancestors to stay alive. Thousands and thousands of years ago it was more important to escape negative situations, often life-threatening experiences, than it was to approach opportunities.

All of this causes wear and tear on our bodies that, over time, can increase our risk of illness. One of the costs of having a distracted and inattentive mind is the extreme activation of the 'stress response'. When you call on this response day in, day out, over the long term the response can accelerate ageing, contribute to poor sleep, affect your appetite and lead to illness, both physical and mental.

shark versus seaweed

fight-or-flight stress response

Breathing rate increases

Heart rate increases

Blood pressure rises

Adrenaline levels increase

Cholesterol levels go up

Immune system is less effective

Anxiety increases

Depression is more prevalent

Sleep disorders increase

Irritability increases

What can we do? There is another response that we can intentionally activate that helps to keep our stress levels down; this is called the relaxation response. In the 1970s, Dr Herbert Benson conducted extensive research on the effects of how we respond to situations – how the stress response versus the relaxation response can affect our bodies. He found that a relaxation response can counterbalance the effects of stress.

The relaxation response has been shown to be the key to increasing motivation, productivity and creativity and improving decision-making ability, as well as lowering stress hormone levels and blood pressure. The relaxation response is perhaps one of the most important skills you can use to gain control over your body. The National Institutes of Health (NIH) in the US recognises the relaxation response as having broad health benefits, including reducing pain and restoring sleep.

The overall goal of the relaxation response is to be physically relaxed and mentally alert. That doesn't mean lying on a sun lounge in Tahiti, or on the couch watching your favourite TV series; nor is it having a sleep. Rather, the relaxation response helps us to reverse the predominant stress response effects, helping us to function in daily life.

shark versus seaweed

relaxation
response

Breathing rate slows down

Heart rate slows

Blood pressure lowers

Adrenaline levels lower

Immune system improves

Sense of wellbeing increases

Sleep improves

Brain wave patterns slow down

Ability to think clearly increases

Increase in creativity and concentration

Our relaxation response needs to be cultivated intentionally, in contrast to the stress response, which is automatic. When we manage our stress response so it only comes out in emergencies, rather than being a daily or even hourly event, we start the process of topping up our personal bank account. Effective, healthy coping skills not only allow you to get through difficult times, they help you to feel calmer and ultimately more confident in your abilities.

The first step to reducing stress is being able to identify the trigger, and recognise what stress feels like in your body. Reflect for a moment on what happens first to your body and then your mind when you feel stressed. Do you feel it in your shoulders? Your breathing? Does your mind feel scattered? Is it hard to focus? Recognising these symptoms gives you insight and allows you to create your own personal go-to, stress-busting tool kit, a structure to support yourself so you can put some space between yourself and the stressor.

how to

Choose one of your stress causes to focus on. How can this situation be changed or improved? For example:

relationship stress

---

assertive communication training,
setting boundaries, resolving conflict

over-commitment

---

setting boundaries, saying no,
eliminating some things from your schedule

grief and loss

---

seeking support, writing in your journal,
finding enjoyable activities to fill your day

Not all stressful situations are within our control, and not every situation can be changed. Effective, healthy coping skills can allow you to get through difficult times.

List three coping strategies that have worked for you in the past that you would like to use regularly:

1. _____

2. _____

3. _____

List three new coping strategies you would like to try:

1. _____

2. _____

3. _____

Assess your current stress levels. How would you rate them on a scale of one to ten (ten being the highest)?

The next step is to create some solutions to help you break the stress cycle. We have put together a list of one-minute sensory stress-busting ideas for you. First, decide which of your five senses is strongest for you; then you can tune in to your favourite sure-fire sensory solution.

sight

Have photos of relaxing places, inspirational landscapes, your next travel destination or people you love close by. We have ours in our diaries so they are always with us. Take a moment to pause and reflect on these.

hearing

Put an audio book, mindfulness app or your favourite music on your phone in advance so you can tune in and tune out.

taste

Have a snack or a cup of tea or coffee (ideally no coffee after 2 p.m. so it doesn't affect your sleep). We don't recommend any alcohol or sugary energy zappers here, sorry!

smell

Take a break to breathe in some fresh air; essential oils can also be a great tool here. Lavender, rose or chamomile are great stress-busting relaxants. You could put a few drops on a tissue and carry that with you or use an oil burner in your home, work or study space.

touch

Put pressure on the points that feel tense in your shoulders or on the palm of your hand near the base of the thumb, as these are go-to points to help release anxiety and tension. If possible take your shoes off and walk in grass. Keep some hand cream handy and take a moment to use it (ideally choose one with essential oils so you can benefit from the aroma – take a deep breath while applying).

Some other healthy coping strategies are below to help you create your go-to stress solution.

healthy coping strategies	unhealthy coping strategies
• Going for a walk, having time in nature, playing golf, riding a bike	• Smoking or drinking too much
• Calling a good friend, booking a regular catch-up	• Over- or under-eating
• Sweating out tension in a workout	• Using drugs
• Listening to music or audio books	• Procrastinating, avoiding facing problems
• Having a massage	• Taking out your stress on others (lashing out, angry outbursts), withdrawing from those closest to you
• Writing in your journal, bathing, lighting a candle	• Zoning out for hours in front of the TV or computer
• Limiting news and media, switching off technology	• Sleeping too much
• Setting boundaries, saying 'no'	
• Resolving conflicts	

A great tool for reducing stress is a simple two-letter word: no. Sometimes the stress we are under is caused by everything we have said yes to; the things we are doing out of guilt rather than because we want to. In other words, it comes from making decisions based on what we think we should do or what we think other people want us to do. If you find it hard to say no, try using 'not today', 'not now' or 'another day' as your go-to 'no' stress busters. We will delve into saying 'no' and your boundaries more in Chapter 10.

Managing your stress is vital to living a healthy, confident life. It lifts the daily burden of guilt, resentment and worry, allowing you to transcend it to approach life in a calm, resilient, relaxed and enjoyable way and create clear pathways for you to thrive in.

'When you arise
in the morning,
think of what a
precious privilege
it is to be alive –
to breathe, to think,
to enjoy, to love.'

marcus aurelius

summary

- Your thoughts automatically activate the stress response.

- The stress response creates wear and tear on your body when activated regularly, rather than when really required.

- The relaxation response is the alternative and needs to be created intentionally.

- Ask yourself: is this a shark or just a piece of seaweed?

- Having a written list of your coping strategies ready is like a first aid kit. Pick your go-to response to stress and be prepared.

- Create space and take a breath before reacting; this will save you a physical stress reaction.

- Stress can be created by over-scheduling ourselves. Learn your best ways of saying no rather than saying yes to everything. 'Not today' or 'not now' can be less confronting than 'no'.

- Don't say you are stressed as it tells the brain to have a physical reaction.

- Having your stress response solution clear will allow you to value your own self-worth, health and wellbeing.

power thoughts

Opportunities often come from challenging situations.

I choose a positive approach.

I have the capability to deal with any challenge.

I am relaxed and free from stress.

I find time each day to relax and unwind.

I let go of tension and stress.

Being calm, relaxed and happy is my natural state.

Today has limitless possibilities.

I can accomplish whatever I set out to do.

I remain calm under pressure.

the
miracle
of breath

create space and clarity

Breathing well is the
skill to master for calm,
confident control
in everyday living.
It links the brain to
the belly and helps you
to relax and stay focused
rather than overthinking
everything, which can
lead to feelings of stress
and anxiety.

the best way to boost your self-confidence when you enter a room for a presentation is to take several deep breaths. The best way to make a decision is to take a breath first, the best way to get to sleep is to breathe consciously first.

Think of seeing a baby asleep and how easily they breathe. A baby's belly is like a balloon, effortlessly rising and falling. As we get older we don't seem to use the full breath that is available to us so readily. When we feel tense or under pressure, our breath becomes shorter and sharper and we breathe mainly from our chests. Chest breathing only uses about half of your lung capacity, as opposed to belly breathing, where you are using your full lung capacity. This fully oxygenates the body, recharging our cells, muscles and organs.

Breathing is something we do every day without thinking about; it is an automatic habit. On average we take around 17000 breaths every day. How many breaths have you noticed today? Most of the time our breath goes unnoticed and yet it is available to us at every moment as a free stress management tool! When the air is clear, your lungs strong, your body relaxed and your mind at peace, you experience total confidence and wellness.

The human body is incredibly adaptive and resilient. We can survive for weeks without food, and for several days without water. But without air, life ceases in only a matter of minutes. Breath is essential for optimum

the miracle of breath

functioning of your brain, your nervous system and all your internal organs. Oxygen is an incredibly valuable and vital nutrient, required for the body to function and to purify the bloodstream of toxins. Every time you take a full breath you are recharging your body just as plugging your phone into a power source recharges your phone.

Controlled, mindful breathing encourages relaxation and helps to cultivate the relaxation response. Many disciplines, such as tai chi and yoga, have long understood the power of breath, and that breath is the link between the mind and the body. Correct breathing now has plenty of science behind it to show that it can help us manage stress and turn off our fight-or-flight reactions by soothing the nervous system, as well as helping to lower our blood pressure and anxiety levels.

A great analogy we use with our clients to encourage them to work on their breathing is a glass of muddy water. When you allow it time to settle and be still, the sediment all sinks to the bottom and you have clear water. By taking the time to reset your breathing throughout the day you allow the mud of your mind to settle, giving yourself a pause and enabling clear, calm, and confident thoughts to flow.

Our minds have no off-switch, but if you give them the chance, they will settle. When you shake up the glass, the water becomes murky, but if you let it sit, the mud settles down and the water becomes clear. This is what happens to your mind with regular focus on your breath. Your thoughts settle down and you can see more clearly what is in front of you, which can lead to clearer thinking, better decision-making and more creativity.

Your emotional health affects the way you breathe. When we are tense or stressed we take shorter, shallower breaths. With full, deep breathing, the ups and downs of the mind can be controlled, making it more relaxed, focused and calm. To get the best out of living in our high-tech, high-achieving, highly pressured modern life, we have to counteract the effects of excessive stress by creating resets during our day to manage and lower our stress.

Your posture also influences how you breathe. The diaphragm cannot do its job of expanding if the abdominal muscles that support it are weak, or if the mid-region is caved in on itself. The body will naturally compensate by breathing predominantly from the upper chest, never fully filling the lungs, resulting in a half-breath or less. Pause for a moment and check your posture. Does it currently enhance your natural breathing or restrict you to a shallow, constrained intake of air?

We are all spending more time in cars, sitting down in transit, sitting at work, sitting on the couch, sitting for lunch. This predominantly seated modern life requires us to have ergonomics at the centre of our thoughts so that we can have a relaxed and aligned posture that supports optimum breathing. We continually do things that restrict our breathing, and changing this pattern requires us to pay attention to it. This can be as small as paying attention to one breath per day to begin with.

Taking the time to reset your breathing throughout the day will enable you to benefit from clear, calm and confident thoughts.

reset

---

creating a simple reset for your breathing can be a great place to start when you're trying to make deep breathing the norm rather than the exception. Linking something you do regularly to your breath can help you to build in a new habit. It can be as simple as these ideas:

- every time you put your phone on the charger take one deep breath;
- upon waking take three deep breaths before getting out of bed;
- or when you go to bed take five deep breaths before falling asleep.

Over time this will have a cumulative effect on you and before you know it you will be taking deep breaths throughout the day without noticing. These resets allow you to manage your stress levels and build in foundations of feeling calm and grounded. They start to train your body into an automatic habit.

'You cannot breathe
deeply and worry
at the same time.
Breathe.
Let the worry go.
Breathe.
Allow the love
and intuition in.'

sonia choquette

'I like to use daily routines every day to remind me of my breathing. Every time I use my body wash in the shower I take a deep breath and really notice the aroma of the essential oils, which are also having a great benefit on my mind. At work I have my essential oil on my desk as my reminder to stop and take a deep breath. Simply opening the bottle throughout the day and taking one or two deep breaths helps me to breathe more deeply, more often, so it becomes a more automated habit. You can do this with your daily coffee or hand cream.'

shannah kennedy

Our days are made up of approximately 40 per cent habit, so the more we can automate our good habits, the less our brain needs to process information and it can get on with giving your highest value contribution to whatever it is you are passionate about.

So the next time you are stuck in a traffic jam, don't grit your teeth and tighten your grip on the steering wheel; exercise your ribcage with some deep breathing and let go of the build-up of tension with long exhalations. It doesn't have to be a chore; simply start with one deep breath a day and from here you can build on your practice to become a foundation of your personal stress management skill set.

tense breathing	relaxed breathing
From the chest	From the belly
Longer in breaths (holding at the top)	Longer out breaths (resting at the bottom)
Tight and jerky	Soft and flowing

chaos to calm

how to

The fastest way to start relaxing is to consciously sigh. It reverses almost all the signs of tense breathing. The big in-breath opens the tight chest muscles. The most time-efficient meditation you can do is called 'the three sighs'. It takes about twenty seconds and is a classical spot meditation that is versatile and portable.

the three sighs

Put your left hand on your belly and your right hand on your chest.

Take three slow, deep breaths.

Feel your left hand rise and fall, and sigh on the exhalation.
(There should be hardly any movement in your
right hand as you breathe.)

Lengthen and align your spine to allow your lungs to fill with oxygen.

Breathe in deeply, and this time sigh on the out-breath.

Take another deep breath in and sigh.

Repeat.

Breathe naturally.

Take a deep breath and bring your awareness back to the present.

Feel what it feels like to be breathing using your full lung capacity.

one-minute breathing for muscle release

Take some long, slow, deep breaths.

As you breathe in feel your belly rise,
and as you breathe out, feel your belly fall.

Now take your awareness to your shoulders and with
every out-breath, allow your shoulders to relax,
releasing any tension.

Move your awareness to your jaw and facial muscles
and with every out-breath allow your jaw and
facial muscles to soften and relax.

These are simple techniques that are portable and easy to use. The breath connects you back to your true, authentic self. It assists in slowing down the engine of your brain so you can take some control and step off the treadmill of life for a moment.

Deep breathing is a great way to stay calm and focused during the day. It's all about the small steps to success – one deep breath is better than none. Take a pause during the day and integrate the breathing trigger that works best for you.

Inspire: a breathing in, as of air into the lungs; inhaling.

2. an inspiring or being inspired mentally or emotionally.

3. an inspiring influence; any stimulus to creative thought or action.

Webster's New World Dictionary, Second College Edition

Surprised to learn that the first dictionary definition
of 'inspiration' has to do with breathing?
Yet how appropriate. And how interesting that
together, the definitions of this word mean
to take air in and then be stimulated into creativity!

summary

- Our breath is free and available, and it only requires our attention to utilise its full capacity.

- The breath calms our minds and bodies.

- One deep breath per day is better than none.

- Over time, build more breathing resets into your schedule to manage your stress and feel calm.

- Relaxed and aligned posture supports optimum breathing.

- Check the ergonomics of your car, desk, dinner tables and lounges to remove any obstacles to full breathing.

- Make breathing consciously a habit when you are in the car, in the shower or brushing your teeth.

- Altering your breathing quickly alters your mood, and developing good breathing habits can improve vitality, better health and calm.

- Becoming skilled at changing your state through altering your breathing boosts your confidence in your ability to manage yourself so that unwelcome moods become just that – unwelcome. Not fearful, threatening, or indicative of personal weakness or inadequacy.

power
thoughts

When I breathe, I let go of panic.

The more I breathe, the happier I am.

When I breathe, I am calm and at peace.

The more I breathe, the better I feel.

Focusing on my breathing makes
me feel relaxed and calm.

I breathe deeply every day.

I am a relaxed person.

I improve my mood by breathing mindfully.

My breathe calms my mind and body.

I breathe easily and naturally.

connect
your
power

---

know your strengths

Our strengths are
our internal compass;
without any effort they
are there, ready for
us to tap into to make
our path easier and
more enjoyable.

We can spend so much of our time on the merry-go-round in our minds, churning over our weaknesses and focusing on how we can overcome them. Rather than spending time in this unrewarding thought pattern there is now strong evidence to show there is much more to be gained from focusing on your strengths and tapping into them as often as possible.

For example, if you love decorating, shopping for new outfits and changing around rooms, your strength may be creativity, detail, and an appreciation of beauty. If you love going through new ideas with people, discussing plans and getting things done, your strength may be relationships, planning and strategic thinking.

Natural strengths are the parts of us that we don't have to do anything to get; they are already there and we can call upon them during our day-to-day experiences of life. Additional strengths are generally something we've learned, shaped by our environment, our experiences and the values with which we identify and choose to live by. We all have a collection of strengths that make up our unique architecture; getting to know your strengths unlocks the confident and competent part of us that thrives in high flow.

You might be asking yourself 'What's the benefit of my particular strength?' The reason these strengths are so exciting is that we are able to access that state of flow – you know the feeling when you lose track of time, when you are lost in the moment, when tasks are neither too hard nor too easy. When we use our greatest strengths we tend to go into flow more often.

When we are in the flow, whatever we are doing becomes more effortless and enjoyable. This means, for example, if you are able to tap into your strengths at work, it is more likely not only to be a sustainable career choice, you will also enjoy it more and thrive. When we are absorbed and engaged, we perform at our best, which then boosts our confidence and makes us feel motivated and energised. This means we are more likely to participate in life (rather than becoming alienated from it), to enjoy activities (rather than finding them dreary), and to have a sense of empowerment (rather than helplessness).

During the last decade there have been many papers and books written in the field of positive psychology on personal strengths – how to spot them and why we should use them. A set of twenty-four main strengths has been identified in the research of Dr Martin Seligman at the University of Pennsylvania and the late Dr Chris Peterson at the University of Michigan. They found that these character strengths, in their different combinations, help people flourish. We all have these twenty-four strengths in different combinations that are unique to us, and that are important for us to flourish as individuals. However, a strength, or a character skill, is something you can work on and improve. Tapping into our strengths will make all the tasks or activities we engage in more pleasurable, and more effortless.

In 2008, positive psychology researcher and entrepreneur Alex Linley released the book *Average to A+: Realising Strengths in Yourself and Others*. Linley found that utilising your strengths resulted in higher

'Be yourself;
everyone else
is already
taken.'

---

oscar wilde

levels of happiness, wellbeing, and fulfilment. When you know your strengths, you gain access to what you already have at your fingertips. With this insight you can align your career, hobbies and relationships in the way that has the greatest meaning, sustainability and purpose for you. In contrast to strengths, our weaknesses drain us and can leave us feeling unmotivated, depleted and tired. A great reason to avoid these wherever possible.

If your top strength is teamwork, then look to ways you can utilise this strength in all aspects of your life. A solo career is probably not for you. You could consider ways to utilise teamwork more at work, in your family, with friends and perhaps by playing a sport or joining a musical group. Think back to when you have been in team environments and you were flourishing. What were you doing? How did other people respond? How could you have more teamwork in your life?

For example, Lyndall's top strength is self-regulation. 'Self-regulation is a form of discipline; it is my ability to self-consciously regulate what I feel and what I do without outside help. I utilise this strength in many areas of my life, from business achievements through to getting up consistently at 5.30 in the morning to exercise. For most people, getting up at that hour is more torturous than pleasurable. When I was growing up on the farm, the day began early and I thrived on this, obviously tapping into my strength. I have continued this habit through my life; getting up and going for a run, doing yoga or exercise in the early morning taps into my strength of self-regulation and I find

Knowing your constellation of character strengths is the first step towards living a happier, more authentic life.

it both effortless and motivating. I use this to be disciplined in what I eat and how organised I am in my life. Like everything, too much self-regulation is something I need to be careful with as pushing myself beyond my limits or further than I can sustain is not going to be a good use of my strengths. Like everything in life, a balance of both is ideal, as self-regulation is a resource that can be depleted and fatigued. A useful metaphor can be that self-regulation acts like a muscle, which can be exhausted through over-exertion or strengthened through regular practice.'

Here are some exercises for boosting self-regulation:

- Next time you get upset, make a conscious effort to control your emotions and focus on positive attributes.
- Set goals to improve your everyday living (for example, room cleaning, laundry, doing dishes, cleaning your desk) and make sure you complete the tasks.
- Pay close attention to your biological clock. Do your most important tasks when you are most alert.

how to

Take a look at the list below. Which three words best represent your strengths? Then think about which three words your closest friends might choose to describe you. Are they the same?

Creative	Self-regulator
Perceptive	Team player
Critical thinker	Humble
Curious	Analytical
Honest	Communicative
Brave	Empathetic
Fair	Independent
Humourous	Wise
Persistent	Strategic
Kind	Confident
Leader	Intelligent
Grateful	Spiritual

1. **Focus on your top three strengths.** The best way to do this is to reflect on 'defining moments' in your career, relationship and life (i.e., times when you felt particularly engaged and inspired, and you were truly at your peak). What did you learn about yourself and your strengths? What type of work or hobby do you find really energising and confidence boosting? How can you secure more of this type of work in your current job or elsewhere?

2. **Develop new skills** that build on your strengths and will help you achieve your goals. If creativity is one of your strengths, think about how you can use this strength daily. Think about ways to tap into this skill set you already have.

3. **Maintain balance.** Be aware that every strength can have a negative effect if it is overplayed. For example, critical thinking can be a wonderful strength for helping you make decisions; however it can also be detrimental if you judge yourself and those around you harshly.

4. **Utilise your strengths.** Whenever you find something challenging, think of your strengths and how you can use those skills immediately to make the next step easier. Remember that most success is not built overnight. It takes concerted effort, disciplined execution and, finally, decisive action to grab 'Lady Luck' firmly with both hands.

In the quest to magnify your inner voices of strength and opportunity and lessen the voices of self-doubt and self-criticism, tapping into your strengths is a foundational tool. Remember the quote of the first man to reach the summit of Mount Everest, Sir Edmund Hillary: 'It is not the mountain we conquer but ourselves.' Try answering these questions to learn more about your strengths and think about how you could use them to enhance your confidence and happiness.

Do your signature strengths match up with those used in your job?

_____

If not, could you adjust your job so that they do? Or perhaps even change your job?

_____

How do your strengths fit with the strengths of those closest to you, such as your partner if you have one, or close friends?

_____

Which strengths give you the most energy when you use them? How could you use them more?

_____

How could you use your strengths differently – say in a different context or with different people?

_____

What hobbies/interests do you have and how do your strengths contribute?

_____

Are there other interests you could develop on the basis of your strengths?

_____

When you last felt a strong sense of confidence, what strengths were you tapping into?

_____

Start working with your strengths, get clear on what they are and flow with them. Your confidence tank will refuel in no time.

summary

- Our strengths are available to us at any time.

- Our strengths are our internal compass.

- When we use our strengths at work
our jobs become more enjoyable.

- Our strengths highlight an engaging,
purposeful, confident path.

- Identify your top three strengths
and think of creative ways to tap into them.

- You can develop your strengths with awareness;
focus on these rather than your weaknesses.

- When you hit that state of flow, you are using
your strengths in action.

- Build new skills with your strengths.

- You can experience higher levels of happiness,
fulfilment and wellbeing when you use your strengths.

power thoughts

I believe in my abilities and my strengths.

I accomplish everything I set out to do in life.

I have faith in myself and in my abilities.

My strengths and talents will help me to realise my dreams.

I love discovering abilities that
I didn't know I possessed.

My strengths and abilities are unique to me.

I recognise and appreciate my talents, abilities and skills.

I respect my abilities and I always fulfil my potential.

My confidence in myself increases daily.

I have total confidence in my strengths and abilities.

discover
what
matters

cement core values

Getting clear on your
own set of values enables
you to make calm,
confident decisions.
Values allow you to be
true to yourself and
love with authenticity.
Values are what matter
to you most and they
influence our personal
attitude, outlooks
and behaviours. Values
are the underlying
motivators of our life.

I n today's world, many people are influenced by advertising, social media and peer-group pressure, defining their true worth by comparison to others. We judge ourselves by acquired material values such as net monetary worth, personal possessions, cars, homes, clothes, external appearance and extravagant holidays. This misrepresents the source of our true worth. So many people lack confidence due to a culture focused on accumulation.

Remember that everyone is different, so discovering what is truly important to you will serve as a great foundation for your life, helping you feel in control, confident and fulfilled so you can experience a great sense of wellbeing. A life with some simple defined values is a life of self-respect and dignity. Clearly defined values bring independence and freedom, expand our ability to be self-sufficient and help free us from negative external influences.

When we recognise, connect, appreciate and work with our own inner ideals and consistently apply them to our daily life and decision-making with positive thoughts and intentions, our lives will be filled with an inner confidence and feeling of self-worth.

Knowledge of our own set of values offers protection from the barrage of external influences and brings a sense of empowerment. The process of understanding our values invites us to go within and cultivate an inner awareness of what is truly valuable to us. If you strip life back to its bare

discover what matters

bones, you will see what is fundamentally important to you. When you are aware of your values, own them and are confident with them, you will manifest opportunities in these areas and move away from destructive decisions and habits.

Discovering your personal values involves finding out not just what you're passionate about but also what's really important to you. The best day of your life is the one on which you decide to own your own set of values and live by them. Your values are an unwavering belief in what you stand for. When you know your values, you can live a happier life doing what's most important to you.

benefits of knowing your values

- Your values influence your behaviours, your choices and your emotions.
- Your values influence your habits, your lifestyle and your social experiences.
- Your values serve as the foundation for confident decision-making.
- Your values define your self-worth and steer you in the right direction for a fulfilled life.

When you look in the mirror each morning to connect with yourself, set up your daily focus and practise some gratitude, your values can be used as a base. If you know what is truly important to you, then you have a solid foundation to feel confident.

Shannah says, 'My values are health, family happiness and achievement. They are rock solid and assist with all my decision-making. Focusing on my values is simple, fast and effective, and it allows me to be authentic and do what is best for my life. Health – physical, mental and emotional – I hold as my first value. Each day when I look in the mirror I can connect with this, question and plan. For example, when I am asked to go to another function, party or dinner, if I have enough in my diary, then saying no is easy and effortless. Saying yes will tip my health the wrong way, as I live with chronic fatigue and need to ensure that my health comes first. The result of not being true to myself here is fatigue and resentment; I cannot enjoy my exercise, family my work, so putting my health first is easy as it has been defined as a value.

'Family happiness is vital for me. That does not mean my family is happy all the time. It means looking at who am I being in the family. Am I being the best version of myself as a wife, mother, daughter, friend and so on? I want to be a fun and inspiring wife, and a warm, nurturing and fair mother. I need to practise this. If I am tired, or find myself on the wrong trains of thought, or not affirming what I want to be, then I am not happy and the family is not happy. So ownership of this is critical. I ask for help when I need it, I read books on parenting, I employ a coach when in need and I stay true to being the wife my husband married. This is a lifelong commitment and some days I get it totally wrong! But I always reset and move forward.

'Achievement is how I am wired: I'm a type A overachiever. This, when not understood, is not healthy, and leads to problems. Perfectionism creeps in and robs me of happiness. Many people have stress, anxiety and low self-confidence, believe it or not, as they have not come to terms with healthy achievement, but rather based their sense of achievement on smashing goals, making money or getting their directorship. I need achievement every day. So I have had to make my understanding of achievement work for me. Taking time out, doing a meditation, sitting still and alone is a big achievement that I now value as much as giving a speech to 300 people. Turning off, switching off technology and insisting on as many 'family at the table' dinners as possible is an achievement that I value just as much as getting another deal. It took me a while but I am much healthier now with this attitude.'

It is the simple things that support our values. If you are creative, what creativity are you bringing into your daily life? You don't necessarily have to go on art retreats; you can be creative with your cooking, your finances, your relationships. If family is a value, then ask yourself, what are you doing for your family? Do you smile when you walk in the front door and treat them as if they are the most important meeting of the day? Do you take time to listen more than speak? Do you add your opinion or wait until you are actually asked to give it? Do you add some spice and value to your family?

Identifying your three most important values keeps you confident and self-assured, and most of all, it can help to keep life simple and calm.

how values grow confidence

Our values are fundamental to help us gain confidence and clarity in our decisions about what matters most to us, and ultimately help us live a happy and successful life. Through understanding your values you will be able to prioritise effectively, make consistent decisions and take action in a way that leads you to success and happiness in the areas you pursue.

'Your beliefs
become your thoughts,
Your thoughts
become your words,
Your words
become your actions,
Your actions
become your habits,
Your habits
become your values,
Your values
become your destiny.'

mahatma gandhi

how to

To help you work out your values, think about when you were your most confident, happy and fulfilled. What was most important for you at that time?

1. **Select** Identify your top ten values, choosing from the box to the right. Don't spend too much time agonising over your decisions: go with your gut instinct.

2. **Prioritise** Prioritise each value from one to ten. Focus on your top five and briefly define what each one means to you.

3. **Contemplate** Read each value slowly, letting the meaning of each word sink in so that you fully understand what each one means to you.

4. **Define** Select your top three values and write them down. Commit them to memory, as they will now act as your decision-making blueprint. You also need to define the single value that is most important to you.

5. **Commit** Work out what you need to add or remove from your life and what you need to change to reflect these values.

Family happiness quality time, bonding	**Self-respect** sense of personal identity, pride	**Generosity** helping others, improving society
Competitiveness winning, taking risks	**Recognition** acknowledgement, status	**Wisdom** discovering and understanding knowledge
Friendship close relationships with others	**Advancement** promotions	**Spirituality** strong religious and/or spiritual beliefs
Affection love, caring	**Health** mental, physical	**Loyalty** devotion, trustworthiness
Cooperation working well with others, teamwork	**Responsibility** being accountable for results	**Culture** traditions, customs, beliefs
Adventure new challenges	**Fame** public recognition	**Inner harmony** being at peace
Achievement a sense of accomplishment	**Involvement** belonging, being involved with others	**Order** stability, conformity, tranquillity
Wealth getting rich, making money	**Economic security** strong and consistent income streams	**Creativity** being imaginative, innovative
Energy vitality, vim, vigour	**Pleasure** fun, laughter, a leisurely lifestyle	**Integrity** honesty, sincerity, standing up for oneself
Freedom independence, autonomy	**Power** control, authority or influence over others	**Personal development** use of personal potential

What are your three most important values?

1. _____

_____

2. _____

_____

3. _____

_____

Write a sentence to describe what each value means to you. For example, if one of your values is health, your sentence could be something like: 'I need to feel physically strong and flexible, to be in positive mental health and feel emotionally supported.'

1. _____

_____

2. _____

_____

3. _____

_____

What do you need to add to your life to reflect these values?:

1. _____

_____

2. _____

_____

3. _____

_____

What do you need to change or get rid of to reflect these values?:

1. _____

_____

2. _____

_____

3. _____

_____

Make sure these values feel right to you, at your core. Do they make you feel supported and confident? Will they assist with how you make decisions?

fill your tank with your values

To keep your values in mind,
working as your foundation, write them
down in some or all of the following ways:

On a post-it note on your car dashboard

On your mirror

Next to your bed

As your screensaver

As a daily reminder on your devices

On the fridge

As a visual in words or pictures, hung up
somewhere you can see it daily

now that you know your values, it is time to allow them to fill your confidence tank. Use them as your foundation. Just like a business has its set of values and a mission statement, use these as yours. When faced with a decision, ask yourself, 'Will this add to my values, or detract from them?'

When we learn a new skill we need to see it and practise it daily so it becomes a habit. With values, we need to see them and read them every single day for our confidence and wellness journey to work well. Shannah's morning ritual is to say her values out loud before she even gets out of bed, and she sets herself an intention for the day that supports them. Her diary is planned each day with some activity or acknowledgement around her values.

summary

- Consciously knowing and living by our values is a skill.

- Values act as our compass to put us back on course every single day.

- Values simplify decision-making in our lives
  so we can stay on track authentically.

- Make a visual picture board or word art of your own set of values.

- Values are a base for confident decisions,
  which in turn will help the way you feel about yourself.

- Post sticky notes of your values on your mirror or car dashboard,
  and make sure you can see them daily.

- Walk the talk. Actively make decisions that
  integrate your values and your actions.

- Use the words: 'I choose to _____ ' instead of helpless phrases like
  'I can't because _____ ' or 'I am like this because of _____ '.
  You have a choice. You decide the circumstances.

- Learn to say 'no' when opportunities arise
  that take you away from your values.

- By making a life according to your key values,
  you can minimise the stress and anxiety
  in all areas of your life.

power thoughts

All areas of my life are in balance with my values.

My values keep my life on course.

My actions support my life values.

All my goals are in keeping with my values.

All my thoughts and words support my values.

Identifying my values gives my life purpose and meaning.

My actions reflect the values that are important to me.

I acknowledge my values in all that I do.

I acknowledge that other people's values are as valid as my own.

I act with confidence because I am guided by my values.

dare
to
dream

---

create your future map

So what's the secret
to reaching your goals
and living the dream life
you've always imagined?
The answer is simple:
it is all about choices.
We make choices every day
that affect, guide and
steer us towards success.

just imagine you are piloting a plane; it is on the runway and needs a flight path for you to know how much fuel it will need before you can take off. Similarly, without a vision your life can feel as if you don't have a flight path and you are just existing without purpose or direction, or in other words, just sitting on the tarmac.

Many of our clients have no plan for the future. They cannot think about what they want six months down the track as they are just living and reacting to life, rather than making the most of the opportunities it presents. This feeling can be compared to being in the passenger seat rather than in the driver's seat, or to just driving in circles around a roundabout, unsure of which exit to take. Clarity about where you are going gives you a big boost of confidence, inspiration and motivation as you have a pathway to move forward on. An example we've seen is that many professional athletes have plenty of vision while they're working as athletes, but lack one for after their sporting career and often find themselves feeling lost.

A good healthy vision, based on your values, is what drives your decisions and actions, which in turn support the foundation of confidence. You can make informed choices as you have already thought things through and become familiar ahead of time with the path you are taking. It is not so much about what *should* happen, but what *could* happen if you are open to growth and evolving as a person.

There is information all around us; ideas that motivate us, uncover our potential and excite us. A confident vision allows us to feel quiet harmony in knowing that we have taken the time to think about what we want in life. A vision for the future will help us to be calm, happy, healthy, confident and inspired.

A client of ours, Robyn, had no vision. She was working hard, and was a single mother trying to fit everything in. She felt trapped, as if this would be her life forever, and she'd fallen into some bad habits with no sense of ownership over any of them. She was existing day-to-day and felt as if she was on the time-poor treadmill of life. After spending some time thinking about her vision of what she really wanted her future to look like, how she wanted to feel, where she wanted to live, and what type of person she wanted to be, she got excited about taking responsibility for her life and making some changes. She booked in her holidays at work six months ahead of time so she had plenty to look forward to; she started to say no to opportunities that really were just distractions, and made decisions that were less self-sabotaging. Her vision board excited her and helped keep her on track to making the change back to the simpler, more empowered path she wanted to be on. Opening her mind up and allowing some creativity in allowed her to move house, change her job to an area that she was genuinely interested in and create some time to be the mother she so wanted to be. Robyn was soon flourishing and filled with confidence and happiness.

A vision is not just a picture of what could be; it is an appeal to our better selves, a call to become something more.

You decide: do you want simply to exist, or to make the rest of your life the most productive, exciting and satisfying years you've ever had? We suggest starting with a three-year plan.

create your own confident three-year vision

Start thinking about who you want to evolve into and how you see yourself living. Be bold! Decide what you want most in life, so you can plan how to obtain it or feel it.

Where will you be three years from today?

_____

_____

My age in three years is:

_____

My partner's, children's, parents' and pets' ages in three years' time are:

_____

dare to dream

my three-year vision is ...

Write down whatever comes to mind, without being held back by fears. Imagine you're not limited by lack of money, skills or time. This is a list of the hopes and dreams you're carrying for the next three years of your life. Remember to focus also on how you feel, not just what you think. For example: 'I will feel confident when I am in control of my money, with a system that supports me and I understand my decisions in spending, saving and wealth creation.'

powerful thought starters

- Who inspires you and why?
- What and who are most important to you?
- How do you want to be remembered?
- If you were mindful of the golden moments in your life, what would you see?
- What kind of work do you want to be doing? How do you feel about this work?
- How much money will you be earning? What are you doing with it?
- What's your health like? How are you getting these outcomes?
- Who brings you joy in your life? How do you spend your time together?
- What are you learning? What difference is this making in your life?

- What do you do for fun? Do you have a hobby or a passion project? Are you travelling?
- Where do you want to live? What makes this feel like a haven?
- What do you want your living environment to look like?
- Who do you want in your social circle? Who inspires and supports you?
- How will your core values be fulfilled?
- What will your purpose in life be?
- How will your finances be managed?
- What do you need to keep doing to keep your confidence at a healthy level?
- Who do you want to be in the family? How do you want to act and be around them?

Now you have some knowledge of what you want to create. You have ideas, inspirations and statements that excite you. Write a few paragraphs to capture this knowledge, exploring how you want to feel, look and act. Write as if it is actually happening, in the present tense. This will connect you emotionally with where you want to go. Watch the world open up to you after you do this activity. Your efforts will no doubt be rewarded as your decisions, in alignment with your values, will get you there.

create a vision board

Creating a vision board is a wonderful technique for manifesting goals and is one of the most powerful tools you can use to boost your confidence and take control. Statistics show that we retain 75 per cent of what we write down. If the first step to achieving a goal is to remember it, then that's obviously a very important step. Learning consultants also say that most of us are more likely to retain ideas if we visualise them. Vision boards are a great way to turn your dreams into something you can see. Take the time to dream and plan and give yourself permission to aim high and be creative. Create a visual document of your three-year plan. Get some board and cut and pin pictures, words and affirmations that will move you forward in the direction you want to take your life.

Many highly successful people use this technique. Feel your way through this exercise rather than thinking. If you take too much time looking for 'ideal images', you might find that perfectionism gets in your way. If you never make time to complete the exercise, you might find that you spend so much time taking care of everyone else's needs that you neglect your own. And don't put anything on your board that isn't extremely appealing to you.

Whatever we focus on, we give energy to. If we focus on stress, we get stress. If we want joy, we need to feel and acknowledge it when there is joy; if we want wellbeing we need to feel and focus on wellbeing. What are you envisioning for the next year of your life? Our unconscious minds work in pictures, so it is time to get creative and own the story with which you want to move forward.

Some examples include: pictures of places you would like to travel to, your favourite car, your dream lover, your dream body, your business goals, inspirational quotes, pictures of friends and family – really, anything that you love and are grateful for. It is so exciting to look at your vision board, to be open to abundance around it and to let opportunity come in. It sparks a feeling of being the driver in life, a feeling of purpose and clarity in direction, which in turn leads to filling our confidence

'Vision without action is a daydream. Action without vision is a nightmare.'

---

japanese proverb

tank. If you like quiet space, put up pictures of nature to fuel your soul: beaches, nature walks, plants that grow and develop and blossom. They will inspire you to create some quiet space in your life, and growing in your practice of this each day is what will make you calm and confident.

Remember, you don't make a vision board so you can become obsessed by the images, but rather to have a pleasant glimpse into the future that awaits you when you are being true to yourself and living confidently. Just putting the vision board together will make you think about what you want out of life. Looking at it frequently will keep those intentions from fading from your mind. And you can update your vision board whenever you feel the need to re-imagine your life or solidify your goals.

Once you have your board up:

- Look at it regularly. It will give you daily inspiration.
- Read any affirmations or inspirational quotes you've posted aloud.
- Visualise yourself living the life that your board represents.
- Be grateful for the good in your life.
- Look at your board first thing in the morning and right before going to bed.

successful people who use these techniques

spanx creator sara blakely

Sara Blakely talked about using visualisation to become successful in a speech she gave at the Women's Leadership Exchange, an organisation that runs conferences for businesswomen. Blakely explained that her goals were to be self-employed, to invent a product that she could sell to a lot of people, and to create a business that would be able to fund itself. She wrote her goals down and they became reality.

ellen degeneres

There's an episode of *Ellen* where she shows the audience her vision board about her dreams of being on the cover of *Oprah*. For nearly every issue Oprah had been the cover girl, and then Ellen got her dream.

beyoncé

Queen B has a picture of an Academy Award right near her treadmill that she looks at daily so she can keep her goals literally right in front of her.

john assaraf

A succesful entrepreneur and brain researcher who built multiple multi-million-dollar companies in the areas of internet software, real estate, life and business coaching and brain research, Assaraf was featured in the movie *The Secret*, in which he credited a lot of his success to his vision boards. In fact, John had been making vision boards for years when he made one with his dream home on it. Five years later he realised that he had moved into the actual home depicted on his vision board without even knowing it.

summary

- The best day of your life is the day you decide your life is your own.

- Choose your values and create a path for them to grow and evolve by creating a vision for yourself.

- Having a vision for yourself will put you in the driver's seat of life, with inspiration and motivation.

- Having a clear vision will help you attract more of what you want in life and less of what you don't.

- Know where you are going by gaining some clarity and opening your mind up.

- A vision will help you understand your purpose and what you want in life.

- Think big when crafting your future vision.

- Put pen to paper and write down your exciting dreams.

- Create a three-year plan by answering the questions in this chapter and imagining where you want to be and how you want to feel in three years' time.

power
thoughts

From my dreams and ideas I can build my future.

There are no limits on my abilities;
no challenges I cannot overcome.

The universe is behind me in all my endeavours,
helping to turn my dreams into reality.

I am filled with energy and joy, ready to be
channelled into brilliant new ideas.

My future has the potential to be whatever I envision now.

I approach my life with joy and self-confidence.

Today is the beginning of the rest of my life
and I can choose the steps I take.

Through cultivating clarity, I can attract the things
that will bring me the greatest happiness.

This life is my own, and by opening my mind
I will find endless possibilities.

make
stuff
happen

_____

confident goal setting

Goal setting is a powerful process for thinking about your ideal future and for motivating yourself to turn your vision of this future into reality.

he process of setting goals will help you figure out what you want to achieve in life. Once you know what you want, you can concentrate your energy on making it happen instead of wasting time on distractions. Having clearly defined goals will help you measure progress, which in turn will help you to stay motivated. You'll also increase your confidence levels as you achieve goals you've set for yourself. It is always a worthwhile pursuit to set yourself the goal of increasing your self-confidence, because it will compound your success. When you believe in yourself, you are more likely to do whatever it takes to achieve your goals.

Having a road map for the future is crucial to success. Most people we coach need to work on their vision for themselves and on clear and concise goal setting. It's common for people to over-complicate the whole process. Your goals do not have to be major, life-changing feats. They can be as small as committing to taking one deep breath every day, or going for a walk every Saturday, even if it is raining. Small daily acts are often the most powerful of goals and offer the greatest rewards.

There are many methods for goal setting; this chapter outlines some of our favourite tips.

how to

An effective technique is to set just three goals per year that support your values and your three-year vision, and fulfil three basic criteria, which we call the ABC:

achievable

The goal should be both challenging and realistic; for example, 'I will commit to coming home every day and treating my family as if seeing them is the most important meeting of my day; I will make sure the first hour I am home is technology-free time so I can be fully connected to the family. I am confident that I can be in control of technology for this important value of mine.'

believable

As you advance toward your goal, you need to be able to measure your progress easily so that you stay motivated. For example, 'I will commit to updating my finances on the first day of each month. This will give me confidence in life and a feeling of economic security.'

committed

Find a way to commit to your goal; for example, 'I will make better food choices each day to support my physical and mental health. I will prepare my food the night before to ensure my choices support me. This increases my confidence and self-worth.' This gives you a plan you can commit to rather than a vague 'I will eat less junk food'.

'You don't have to
be a fantastic hero
to do certain things –
to compete. You can
be just an ordinary
chap, sufficiently
motivated to reach
challenging goals.'

sir edmund hillary

Set goals with the intention of owning them, acknowledging them and achieving them. For example, 'I will go to the gym every Tuesday, Thursday and Saturday at 6.30 a.m.' Once it is in the diary, you can tick that item off at the completion of each session, feeding your sense of self-worth, accountability and confidence. Most of us don't feel like going to the gym early in the morning, but once it's a 'meeting' in your diary, you're much more likely to do it – and every time you leave the gym you'll feel amazing! As you gain competence, you will also gain self-confidence and become less fearful of failure. Perhaps most importantly, you will discover that committing to your goals helps lead to success.

my goals for this year

Career/business

1. _____

2. _____

3. _____

Health/lifestyle

1. _____

2. _____

3. _____

Family/relationships

1. _____

2. _____

3. _____

Financial/wealth creation

1. _____

2. _____

3. _____

Remember, when we are truly committed to our goals, we achieve them. Often, however, our level of commitment isn't high enough to really get things done. Write your goals down! Put them somewhere you can see them: on the fridge, on the mirror, next to your bed, on a card in your wallet, in the front of your diary.

goals need to be structured

Use your diary. Break down your goals into monthly and weekly incre-
ments and book them in. You can then book in every small action needed
to complete each goal. Every gym session, day for organising finances,
massage, block of study time, holiday flight and date night is booked in.
Try programming your phone to remind you to turn it off for the night,
allowing yourself the space you need to have downtime and prepare
for sleep. Book in appointments such as the dentist, annual medical
check-up and any health-related tests you need so you don't forget. If you
have children or a partner you can book in any of their commitments
you need to be involved in. Doing this will help you feel confident and
in control – in the driver's seat of your own life. You'll feel as if you have
achieved something already, and confident that you've given yourself the
best chance to stick to your goals and feel calm that you have everything
you can mapped out in draft form.

Of course, life will happen; something you haven't planned for will get
in the way occasionally. However, moving the odd appointment is far
less stressful than having no solid structure to support you each month.
This system gives you the best chance to live your best life.

beat procrastination

Every bit of planning, prioritising, and organising comes down to this
simple concept: do the most important task first. Confidence comes
from doing, not procrastinating.

Every great achievement of humankind has been preceded by a long period of hard, concentrated work until the job was done. Selecting your most important task, beginning it, and then concentrating on it until it is complete is the key to high levels of performance and personal productivity. The important tasks are the ones you are most likely to procrastinate on, so tackling them first helps you achieve success.

get confident and celebrate

When you've achieved a goal, take time to enjoy the satisfaction of having done so. Absorb the implications of achieving the goal, and observe the progress that you've made towards other goals. If the goal was a significant one, reward yourself appropriately. All of this helps you build the self-confidence you deserve.

With the experience of having achieved this goal, review the rest of your goal plans:

- If you achieved the goal too easily, make your next goal harder.
- If the goal took a dispiriting amount of time to achieve, make the next goal a little easier.
- If you learned something that would lead you to change the way you approach other goals, make those changes.
- If you noticed a deficit in your skills as you worked towards the goal, decide whether to set goals to fix this.

summary

- Goal setting is a powerful process for thinking about your ideal future, and for motivating yourself to turn your vision of this future into reality.

- ABC – Achievable, Believable and Committed. Use this as your guide.

- Set only three goals per year that you are really prepared to put effort into.

- All goals must be written down. Don't think it, ink it! This crystallises them and gives them more force.

- Set goals with the intention of owning them, acknowledging them and achieving them.

- Structure your goals into your diary, break them down into smaller components, and book them in like appointments.

- Carry your goals with you all day.

- Review your goals each month.

- Express your goals in positive statements.

- Celebrate and feel confident every time you tick off a goal, or action supporting a goal.

power
thoughts

Setting goals is a joyful process.

I let go of any resistance to setting goals.

I write my goals down and review them regularly.

I plan the actions I need to take to achieve my goals.

I have specific goals and action plans.

I visualise the achievement of my goals every day.

I overcome any barriers to achieving my goals.

I set and achieve challenging goals for myself.

My goals are in line with my values.

All of my goals have achievable deadlines.

recipe
for
balance

chart your wellness wheel

When you're juggling
family needs, work
requirements, children
and other commitments,
as well as putting time into
relationships and some
aside for yourself, it can
feel almost impossible to
find the right balance.

W e find that for most of our clients a balanced life can seem out of reach. If we don't have a plan, know where we are and where we want to be, the task can seen insurmountable. Yet, when you get it right, it's very empowering and there's a sense of satisfaction that will keep you coming back for more.

This chapter is going to help you identify where what we call the 'wheel of balance' is for you in four fundamental areas of your life, and then work out where you want to be. Once you have identified this you can start to bridge the gap and set a plan with high-impact, high-reward activities to give you that blissful feeling of balance.

There are four areas of the wheel that form the essential foundations of your personal confidence platform. These are: 'eat', 'move', 'sleep' and 'switch off', and all are vital for solid health, general wellness and confidence. The wellness wheel self-assessment tool (see page 148) helps you look into your life and figure out which areas might be out of balance, preventing you from moving smoothly through changes in your life. It is a tool to help you create positive change so you can feel even happier and more balanced, confident and successful than you already are!

Take some time to reflect on your health, decisions and behaviours. Think of this as a chance to step back and

Small decisions about how you eat, move, sleep and switch off each day count more than you might think.

measure your own life – a basic inventory of your health. The wellness wheel will help you to get a visual representation of the present balance between the four areas of your life, and identify which will most benefit you when you improve them.

Small decisions about how you eat, move, sleep and switch off each day count more than you might think. Making better choices takes effort. Making small, good choices is much easier than struggling to achieve difficult-to-reach ideals, such as 'lose weight' or 'get healthy'. When you have small wins, such as just taking soft drinks out of your diet, or going to bed at 10 p.m. most nights, your confidence and self-belief will flourish and you will be ready to try something bigger.

Let's look at an overview of the four non-negotiable platforms that support you on your way to success.

eat

T here is no one magic eating plan or formula, as every person's body is different. Rather, finding the best way to eat for you is about thinking of food as your fuel source and discovering which fuel works best for your body. Once you have established this, then it's time to set up the structure to support the right eating habits for you.

Eating well and having choices available to you requires preparation and organisation. Often it can be a simple lack of preparation that stops you eating well and means you end up making compromised food choices on the run. A healthy food plan has so many benefits, from raised energy levels, increased productivity, reduced risk of illness, improved mood and better quality sleep. Quite simply, nutrition is essential to good health. If your diet is full of fast foods, takeaways, pre-packaged meals and processed snacks, or foods that don't suit your body, you will struggle to truly nourish your body and give it the energy it needs to perform at its best.

Almost as important as *what* you are eating is *how* are you eating. Are you eating on the run, or taking undistracted time to eat mindfully and allow your body the best opportunity to digest your food well? Or are you regularly eating at your computer, not really thinking about your posture or the speed at which you are eating? It's believed that mindful people are less likely to be overweight, as they take the time to chew, then digest each mouthful. If you are eating mindlessly you will probably eat quickly and then go back for more, not giving your body the time it needs to thoroughly digest your food.

We like to eat by the principles of the 'SLOW' (seasonal, local, organic wholefoods) food movement. The benefits of eating 'SLOW' foods extend beyond your physical health; your food choices are simplified, so you are not mentally distracted by trying to follow diets, fads and ways of eating that just don't suit your body.

S: **Seasonal** Fruit and vegetables that are in season are always the freshest and most nutritious foods. By eating only seasonal produce, you can rest assured that the nutritional content is as good as it gets.

L: **Local** Shopping at local farmers' markets is not only fun, it's inspiring; all the seasonal produce will give your inner cook lots of ideas. Find a farmers' market by checking the Australian Farmers' Markets Association website. There are also many 'farm to you' businesses, as well as fantastic organic and local butchers, and fruit and vegetable shops selling great local and seasonal produce.

O: **Organic** Eating foods that have been produced using organic farming principles minimises your exposure to potentially harmful chemicals. If you're interested in going all the way, you can do this by having your own vegetable garden, compost systems and even chickens if you have the space. It's not for everyone, but it is a great place to start if you are passionate about your food and/or gardening. Otherwise, organically produced foods can easily be found in wholefoods shops, food co-ops, farmers' markets and even the supermarket these days.

W: **Wholefoods** Quite simply, this means eating food that still looks the way it did growing in nature, or very close to it. This is because everything (all the nutrients and fibre) in that whole fruit, vegetable, grain, legume, nut or seed is perfect just the way it is.

recipe for balance

tips for creating more balance

- Drink some water with lemon when you get up each morning to flush your system.
- Put your food on smaller plates – it will help prevent you from overeating.
- Avoid jumping from one diet to the next and focus instead on eating right for life.
- Create a basic list of meals that work for you.
- Put your healthiest snacks at eye level in the fridge and pantry.
- Make sure the basic foods that support you are prepared in advance.
- Have chopped-up vegetable sticks in your fridge for quick snacks.
- Make Sunday your preparation day for the start of the week. What can you prepare in advance to take the pressure off during the week?
- Menu-plan your week so you don't end up aimlessly walking the supermarket aisles, getting distracted.
- Drink 1 litre of water before lunch and 1 litre before 4 p.m. Fill up your bottles the night before so you don't forget.

'To eat is
a necessity,
but to eat
intelligently
is an art.'

_____

francois de la rochefoucauld

move

---

movement not only helps us to feel great, it also reduces the risk of certain diseases, helps us to manage our weight and gives us a better night's sleep. Many of us now live such sedentary lives, there's even a term for it: 'seated living'. Basic, everyday movement is slowing down due to the way we live. Movement is essential to the way you feel in your body. Are you feeling as fit, strong, flexible and lean as you would like?

Shannah uses her strength of self-regulation to exercise in the morning; she finds it is the best way to start her day. However, for some people, finding the motivation to get moving can be really difficult. There is no fail-safe motivational secret. It is about finding the movement recipe that is right for you.

Think about how much activity you engage in each day. How much would you like to have and what areas you would like to work on?

tips for creating more balance

- Build movement and activity into every hour of your day. Every twenty minutes, try to move for at least two minutes.
- Do yoga or stretch to increase or maintain your flexibility.
- Even twenty minutes of moderate activity each day can significantly improve your mood.
- Walk in the mornings.
- Get off the couch and on to the floor; if you're watching TV, take the opportunity to stretch your body.
- Schedule your movement session like a business meeting.
- Keep your movement session at the same time each day where possible. Our bodies work best when we keep to a regular rhythm.
- When you're struggling to get started, focus on how you will feel at the end of the workout.
- Make sure you include a good variety of exercise, as our brains love novelty. Chose a mix of things such as team sport, yoga, Pilates, cardio classes, swimming, outdoor fitness classes, hiking or skiing.
- If exercising in the morning, get your exercise clothes out the night before so you are committed to your workout when you wake up.
- Set your alarm and put it on top of your exercise clothes – just far enough away so you have to get out of bed (no phones in the bedroom – invest in a good old-fashioned alarm clock!).
- Aim to include a mix of strength, suppleness and stamina exercises in your week.

recipe for balance

sleep

a good night's sleep makes you feel better, but its importance goes far beyond just boosting your mood or banishing under-eye circles. Adequate sleep is a key part of a healthy lifestyle, and can benefit your heart, weight, mental health, brain function and more. Sleep deprivation can kill your motivation, make you gain weight gain, affect your mood, make it hard to cope with stress and to concentrate, lower your immunity and increase your risk of serious disease.

Sleep is without question a fundamental part of feeling healthy, confident and able to cope in life. We need good-quality sleep to recharge and re-energise our bodies. Sleep is an essential, non-negotiable foundation of health, giving us clarity, energy and focus. It's ideal to go to bed by 10 or 11 p.m. at the latest. This might mean you need to give yourself a curfew. The hours before midnight are said to be worth double the hours after it, in terms of sleep quality and the benefit to your health. It is during the deepest part of sleep – often the first few hours – when your body replenishes itself and fixes whatever is out of balance. Arianna Huffington, in her book *Thrive*, mentions that she set her alarm clock at night to remind her to go to bed!

You should also think about how you wind down at the end of your day. Are you engaging in sleep-inducing activities to give yourself the best opportunity to sleep well? It is ideal to have at least one hour of technology-free time before bed to allow your melatonin production to kick in and help induce sleep.

Sleep is vital, yet we constantly push ourselves to get by on less and less until we quite often don't even remember what 'peak performance' feels like any more. Treat your bedtime like an appointment, giving it the same priority and importance that you give all your work-related appointments. It is, in effect, a meeting you have scheduled with yourself. It is one of the best tank-fillers you can do, at no cost whatsoever!

tips for creating more balance

- Turn off technology an hour before you go to bed; set an alarm on your phone to remind you to do this each night.
- Get up at the same time each morning, creating a rhythm.
- Make sure your bedroom is 3 to 5 degrees cooler than it is during the day.
- Get at least seven to eight hours of quality sleep each night to stay sharp and achieve more.
- Keep your phone out of the bedroom – buy an alarm clock.
- Your bedroom is your sanctuary, so treat it that way.

switch off

d isconnect to reconnect and get back in touch with yourself. This part of the wheel is about how we intentionally switch off and make use of some self-care strategies. Switching off can be more challenging than staying at work or keeping busy. It involves giving your body the time to rest, and engaging in activities that inspire you. For some, this will start with giving yourself permission to stop; enhancing your happiness and health starts with allowing yourself to feel better, be better and become better. This may sound simple, but it can be a great challenge for many people.When we switch off from our phones and other distracting influences such as computers, television and other devices, we have time to top up our tank of creativity and passion.

We actually have more control over our daily schedules than we like to believe. After we give ourselves permission to be better, we can start taking the reins. Start with small steps; for instance, if you work in an office you could try requesting a trial period of working one day a week from home, or a late morning start so you can do a yoga class. If this energises you, it will enhance your productivity twofold.

More and more businesses now understand that they reap the benefits of allowing employees to work from home, access emails remotely and take fitness classes in the morning. Many of our clients have negotiated for a 4.5 day work week to gain some space, get into their gardens or focus on photography or a hobby. Find the work–life balance that fits you. Self-care is necessary for maximising your energy. Self-care doesn't mean being selfish; in fact, it will help you to help others.

tips for creating more balance

- Create technology boundaries so you switch off.
- Book a massage or other healing act once a month.
- Develop your hobbies: cooking, photography, art, music or crafts.
- Put yourself first and prioritise your time.
- Develop your practice of self-care.
- Immerse yourself in water – have a bath or a swim in the ocean.
- Sit in nature, go for a bushwalk, play golf or work in the garden.
- Book 'your time' in like a business meeting.
- Read a book, newspaper or magazine.
- Meditate, colour in, do a jigsaw.

recipe for balance

how to

Use the illustration of the wheel below to create your own 'wellness wheel'.

1. The centre of the wheel is 0 per cent and the outside is 100 per cent.
2. Place an A on each segment for where you are today.
3. Then place a B on each segment of the wheel for where you would like to be.
4. Then join all the As in a circular way.
5. Then join all the Bs in a circular way.
6. Look at the gap between each segment and write down what is your first priority for each section of your wheel to get you a step closer to your B.

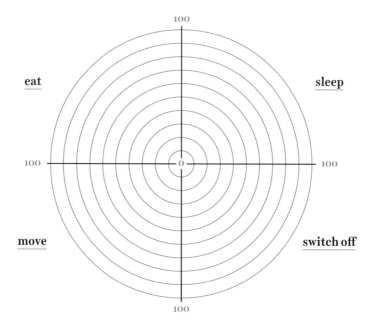

eat _____

_____

move _____

_____

sleep _____

_____

switch off _____

_____

You now have a list of top-priority choices that you can work on and create action steps for.

Now that you have completed your wellness wheel, observe the wheel's shape and balance. How smoothly would it roll? What does it tell you? Does anything surprise you about it? What don't you like about it? What do you like about it?

Remember, every journey begins with a single step. If you can enlist others to travel with you, the journey can be a lot more fun.

summary

- Balancing your wheel results in good health
  and wellbeing.

- The four foundations of wellbeing are
  Eat, Move, Sleep and Switch off.

- Wellness is a way of life – a lifestyle you design
  to achieve your highest potential for wellbeing.

- The four areas of the wheel provide the foundations
  for a confident platform.

- Confidence flourishes as we make small changes
  and commitments in each area.

- Change one thing at a time in each area
  of your wellness wheel.

power
thoughts

Every day I feel a complete sense of wellbeing.

I live a balanced and happy life.

I give myself permission to rest and relax.

Every day I celebrate my continued good health.

I live a full and complete life in body, mind and soul.

I am strong, happy and healthy.

I set myself challenging but achievable fitness goals.

I rest well and peacefully at night.

I think positively about all areas of my life.

My actions support my health and wellbeing.

protect the asset

---

set your boundaries

Life with boundaries doesn't mean being rigid or inflexible; instead, having good boundaries creates and cultivates a purposeful life with great meaning and happiness. It allows you to stay in the driver's seat. It means doing the things you deem important and letting go of those you don't want to do. It's moving from FOMO (fear of missing out) to JOMO (joy of missing out).

One of the great benefits of putting boundaries in place is that it affords us the time, space and energy to devote to the things we feel passionate about – the dreams and aspirations that we might have lost sight of over the years. Responsibilities and commitments to others can take over our lives, and people often find themselves feeling overwhelmed, lacking confidence because they feel they have little control.

If you are in this situation, it can feel totally suffocating and consuming. Some people experience it as a lack of clarity, sometimes to a point of severe anxiety. For some, work and life has lost its purpose and meaning and it feels as if the world is against them. Others feel that they expend time, money and brain power looking after other people's needs, wants and desires more than their own and can start to brew a little resentment.

If any of this resonates with you, it might be a great opportunity to have a look at your personal boundaries. So often our boundaries are non-existent or inconsistent with our values, and when we don't set boundaries and maintain them, we can be guaranteed someone else will, whether that is a work colleague, partner or family. Learning to set clear personal boundaries helps us to have a healthy dose of self-worth. It is our way of communicating to others that we have self-respect and will not allow others to define us.

protect the asset

Quite often the people who have trouble with boundaries are those who are deemed to be great givers. A great giver in a working environment can either go to the top or the bottom of the ladder. One of things that distinguishes those who go to the top is that they can put boundaries in place. Getting clear on your boundaries is a highly valuable investment of your time, protecting the asset: you.

People often feel guilty when they start putting their own needs first, or they feel worried or anxious about what others will think of them. It takes commitment and practice.

There are some common complaints we often hear when our clients are feeling burdened. These can be heavy, draining, negative thoughts to carry around, but if you can alter your approach and start taking responsibility, you can start to make some positive choices about how you allocate your time and you will feel more equipped to cope. Some examples:

feeling burdened	taking responsibility
I never have time to do what I want to do.	I don't take time for my needs.
I always end up doing everything myself.	I don't ask for help.
No one appreciates the things I do.	I take on way too much, hoping that someone will notice and tell me how good I am or how grateful they are.
My kids take up all of my time.	I have chosen to make my children's needs more of a priority than my own.

The first step in establishing boundaries is to ask yourself, 'What do I want to be doing and investing my time in?', rather than, 'What do I feel obliged to do?', which eventually creates a toxic sense of resentment. Some of these obligations may include keeping up-to-date on social media, attending the budget-destroying destination wedding of a distant friend, going to every sport game your child plays or attending functions because you feel you have to. Creating and maintaining our boundaries allows us to fill our diaries from a position of what serves us best instead of what we feel we *should* do.

So often our minds are cluttered with both passions and obligations, all vying for a prime position in our thoughts. Sit down, take a breath and just think about all the demands on your time, your energy and your bank account. If you start to feel pressured, then there are probably too many. The first piece to the puzzle is sorting out the absolutely essential, must-do list, from the perceived obligations.

An effective tool when setting boundaries is putting space between you and the decision. Think about how you will feel when the time comes for you to put your commitment into action. If the answer is 'No, I don't want to do that', then say 'no' straight up. You will eliminate plenty of time you'd be spending processing and deciding by just being upfront and honest. Putting boundaries into practice can be tricky if you are a real 'yes' person. It is normal for some people to feel shame, guilt and anxiety initially when they say 'no'; however, once you have done this a few times you will experience the exhilarating

Establishing boundaries that support you is the first step to living the life you want. They will protect you, physically and emotionally.

freedom of owning your schedule, opening up those reserves of time, energy and money to spend on the things and with the people that make you happy.

Boundaries are really like imaginary lines that help you protect yourself, both physically and emotionally. They keep other people's actions and behaviours from hurting, distracting, annoying or imposing on you.

When personal boundaries are underdeveloped or weak, you may not be able to hold your ground in the world and in relationships. Establishing boundaries that support you is the first step to living a life you want. Once you have established your boundaries, it will require commitment to sustain them, but the benefits you reap will create the momentum for you to protect them when the next decision comes your way.

'Half of the troubles of this life can be traced to saying yes too quickly and not saying no soon enough.'

———————————————

josh billings

how to

When does being generous of spirit turn into being a doormat? When does being a can-do person become a problem? These are questions that many contend with as they learn about the concept of having and setting healthy boundaries. It's time to get into some boundary-setting exercises.

1. **Use technology.** Technology can be a great personal reminder system of what's important to you. To help you get into new habits, program reminders into your device. For example, if you would like to leave work at 5 p.m. for your exercise commitment then set a reminder at 4.30 p.m. that asks, 'What do I need to complete to get out of work in thirty minutes?'

2. **What could you say 'no' to today?** Saying 'yes' is easy, and saying 'no' in a graceful way can be really hard for people who are used to saying 'yes'. This is known as the 'pleasing disease' and often starts in childhood. It can turn into what's often called the 'martyr syndrome' and breeds great resentment in our relationships. Ultimately, we create the situation ourselves. Some graceful ways to say 'no' are: 'At the moment I am out of time, can I help you next week?' 'I don't have the time it deserves right now; maybe next week.' 'Thanks for the offer, can you check back with me next time as I am busy this week.' 'Unfortunately, it would come at the cost of something important, so I will need to pass this time; look forward to being there next time.'

3. **Buy yourself time.** Put space between yourself and the decision – when someone asks if you can do something, whether it's personally or professionally, simply respond with 'I will just need to check my diary and get back to you.' Taking time to check your schedule creates some space and reflection as to whether this is where your highest value contribution can be made and if it's something you actually want to do.

4. **Technology curfew.** Choose a time at night when all the technology goes away. How does it feel when someone you are with is checking emails while having dinner or going for a walk? It is about committing to our technology boundary and modelling behaviour to our children as well as ourselves in a society that is quite new to having so much connectedness. Remember that it will help you sleep if you keep technology out of the bedroom. Give your mind and body the space it so needs and deserves and take back your control here.

5. **Morning technology boundaries.** What is the ideal time for you to start checking emails? Our simple philosophy is to check emails when we are in our office chairs and ready to deal with them. If we start checking emails before we get out of bed or soon afterwards, we start to brew a low level of anxiety or feel pressured in our own homes. Technology boundaries give your mind and body time to switch off, calm down and create the foundations for a great night's sleep or great day ahead. Instead of checking emails, you could spend time focusing on your breathing. Ten minutes a day

is enough to help lower stress levels, reducing cortisol and increasing feel-good chemicals. Before getting out of bed, set your intention for the day and beware of time-robbers.

6. Unsubscribe to reduce the information overload. Spend the next month unsubscribing to every piece of digital information that is not essential. You can always subscribe again if you really miss it.

7. Create an absolute 'no' list – this way your brain automatically knows what to do. Some starters could be:

I no longer

- Rush.
- Have notifications turned on for new messages. I choose when I get my mail.
- Feel bad about saying 'no' when 'no' is what's best for me.
- Get caught up in other people's drama.
- Feel an obligation to spend time with family members or friends who choose to live in chaos.
- Go to events that require hours of idle chit-chat.
- Take phone calls during meals.
- Invest time in relationships that aren't aligned with who I am and who I want to be.
- Feel the need to check my email multiple times a day.

To make sure you've covered everything on your 'no' list, here are some questions to to ask yourself regarding boundaries:

- Where do I feel deprived?
- What do I need more of right now?
- What do I need less of?
- What do I want right now?
- Who or what is causing me to feel resentful?
- What am I craving?

Identify three areas in your life where you need to set clear boundaries but have been unable to in the past.

1. _____

2. _____

3. _____

Identify three actions you can take this week to make your boundaries clear to others without offending them.

1. _____

2. _____

3. _____

What has prevented you from setting boundaries in the past?

1. _____

2. _____

3. _____

some points to ponder

- The life skill of setting healthy boundaries is critical to establish. As you become more successful and take on more responsibilities, you will have a greater need to protect your integrity and the things that are important to you.
- Good, solid boundaries free up your time for those you are connected most to in life.
- Your body never lies and will tell you when to speak up, so get some connection going with your belly when making a decision.

'Think about what
you will tolerate.
Where do you
draw the line?
No one can make you
feel inferior without
your consent.'

---

eleanor roosevelt

summary

- Boundaries define who you are and what you are willing to tolerate. They honour your self-respect and your sense of self-worth. They are the deepest act of self-care there is.

- Ask yourself if you suffer from wanting to please others at the expense of your own happiness.

- Boundaries are essential to becoming a healthy adult and balancing your work and personal life effectively. They demonstrate your commitment to self-respect.

- Many of us are people-pleasers and often put ourselves at a disadvantage by trying to accommodate everyone.

- We don't want to be selfish, so we put our personal needs on the backburner and agree to do things that may not be beneficial to our wellbeing.

- Create boundaries around technology.

- The two main types of boundaries are physical and emotional.

- Try going from FOMO to JOMO.

power
thoughts

I have plenty of time for the things that
are most important to me.

I am open and honest about what I can and can't do.

I find it easy to set boundaries and say 'no'.

I respect the boundaries of others.

I create and maintain boundaries that protect and support me.

I am in touch with what I need for a happy and balanced life.

I am confident in my ability to say 'no'.

I am in control of my life.

I communicate my thoughts and opinions with confidence.

Setting boundaries is a normal part of my everyday life.

nail
it
down

---

hardwire your habits

Day in, day out,
our routines are filled
with habits that help us
and others that hinder us.
Habits are the automated
version of ourselves;
they allow us to get
things done without
thinking about them.

Our habits can propel us forward to new experiences and adventure; however, sometimes they can also keep us trapped in a rut. Like rats in a cage going around and around on their exercise wheel, our habits can be so automatic that when we try to change them, before we know it we find ourselves doing the same old thing again. This can fill us with shame and guilt, and allow our harsh inner critic to have a party. Whether the habit has been ingrained in your life for years or it's something new, it is an automated response that you need to address in order to create new habits to help propel you forward, or break old habits that no longer serve you.

For some of us, walking into work can trigger a habitual feeling of stress and pressure; for some, walking in the front door at home can trigger tension. For others, smoking cigarettes, drinking alcohol or eating chocolate when under stress might be a routine habit that just feels too hard to kick. When we resort to using substances or experiences to escape a feeling we don't like, then it is time to try to understand more about our habits. When we know and understand our habits, it gives us power over them and takes us from merely existing to thriving.

The first step in breaking a bad habit is identifying and understanding what the trigger is. What is the trigger when you get frustrated? What is the trigger for having way too many drinks? What is the trigger for eating chocolate every day? What is the trigger that makes you snap at your kids, partner or anyone close enough to you? When we look at what

nail it down

the trigger is for these negative behaviours, it gives us insight into the changes that we need to make. We can use this awareness to identify both good and bad habits. Simply ask yourself:

- What is the bad habit I would like to change?
- What is the trigger for this habit?
- What is the good habit that I would like to embed in my routine?

Taking some time to identify the behaviour at a deeper level will help you work out how to create the best structure to support a new habit. Once you have identified this, you can make this habit sustainable. We are incredibly passionate about creating a structure that supports constructive habits and sustaining them for the long term.

Quite often clients will ask, 'How do I create habits that stick?' We all have an array of daily habits that we have formed over the years that move us forward, such as the basics of getting to work, eating breakfast and cleaning our teeth; however we can also have a list of persistent time-wasting habits that can inhibit and distract us. Forty per cent of our actions every day aren't actual decisions, but habits. The more we can utilise helpful habits in our day, the more we can make room for our other big-picture plans. But how do we go about breaking bad habits and replacing them with new, positive behaviours?

To take action on our bad habits and encourage the good ones, there is a constructive framework that can help to make it easier to understand and change habits. Research has established that all habits are made up of a routine, a reward and a cue. Once the habit is established, if you want to change it, you need to make adjustments to all three elements.

Over time the cue and reward become intertwined and eventually a habit is born.

Cue Make it easy to get your habit started by anchoring it to habits you already have and embedding it in your daily routine. For example, when you put your phone on the charger you could take one deep breath.

Routine Once you've begun, try to spend a reasonable amount of time practising the desired behaviour. For example, commit to taking one deep breath every time you put your phone on the charger for the next month.

Reward Finally, there is a reward, which helps your brain figure out if this particular loop is worth remembering for the future. The reward gives you a hit of dopamine, our 'feel-good' hormone, and creates a memory of a good habit. For example every time you take a deep breath, you feel calmer and know it is reducing your stress; or you could reward yourself by having a massage at the end of the month when you have sustained the new habit.

Once you understand the habit loop, it is time to decide when you should incorporate your new habit into your day. To give yourself the best chance of success, work with your body's natural rhythms. If you are a morning person prioritise the challenging tasks in the morning and support yourself in the afternoon. Plan your day to maximise your self-regulation and your habits will become easier and more sustainable.

Changing some old, ingrained habits can be difficult. Sometimes change takes a long time. Sometimes it requires repeated experiments and failures. And sometimes it is incredibly hard. But this framework is a

nail it down

place to start. Once you understand how a habit operates, you gain power over it, and then you're on your way. Finally, remember that your brain likes novelty. Every now and again change it up and vary the rewards; you will get another boost of inspiration to propel your habit forward.

When you decide on your new habit, you need to take action within the next twenty-four to forty-eight hours to make a change. When a habit emerges, the brain stops fully participating in decision-making. It stops working so hard, or diverts focus to other tasks. So unless you deliberately fight a habit – unless you find new routines – the pattern will unfold automatically. For example:

old habit

Cue Set the alarm for 6 a.m.
Routine Roll over and turn alarm off, tell yourself 'tomorrow I will do it'.
Reward More time in bed (despite low-level guilt and feeling tired even though you had more sleep).

replacement healthy habit

Cue The night before, get exercise clothes out, set the alarm and leave it on your clothes.
Routine Get up, clothes on and out for some exercise.
Reward Book a massage once a month or tick it off your daily to-do list.

'Happiness
is a habit –
cultivate it.'

———————————

elbert hubbard

how to

```
┌─────────────────────────┐
│   do you want to change  │
│        a habit?          │
└─────────────────────────┘
```

the cue	the reward	the routine

Every habit that we have is made up of a cue, a reward and a routine. Identifying the cue is the first step to changing your habits. What is happening around you when you feel the urge to fulfill a bad habit? What did you just do? Where are you and what time is it? There will be at least one thing that is consistent every time you feel the desire to do your habit.

Your habit is bringing you a reward. Working out exactly what need your habit is fulfilling will help you to replace the reward with something else It won't always be the obvious answer! E.g., is your morning coffee habit rewarding you with caffeine? Or do you like the social aspect of going to the cafe with colleagues? Test out different rewards until you have identified what reward you gain from your habit.

Now that you know what triggers your habit, and what is rewarding it, you can create a new routine and a better habit. Tie your cue to a different, and more beneficial reward, and with practice you will soon find you have created a new habit that benefits you.

1. Identify the cue.
2. Experiment with rewards.
3. Create a new routine.
4. Practise.

what is your new habit?

New habit _____

_____

Cue _____

_____

Routine _____

_____

Reward _____

_____

summary

- Your life is essentially the sum of your habits.
- Use the three-step process to break old habits and create new ones.
- There is evidence to show that the 'habit loop' will successfully create habits that stick.
- Once you know the habit loop, you have power over the habit.
- Habits are automated responses we train our mind to make.
- Approximately 40 per cent of our day is made up of habits.
- The more we can program ourselves to automatically carry out constructive habits, the more time we can spend thinking about other, more exciting projects and adventures.
- Vary your rewards to provide novelty and variety.
- Identify your triggers for good and bad habits.

power thoughts

My habits contribute to my calm and confident life.
_____

All my habits are positive and beneficial
to my health and wellbeing.
_____

My habits support me in attaining my goals.
_____

Changing my behaviour is as easy as changing my thoughts.
_____

I control my habits rather than letting them control me.
_____

I develop new and positive habits regularly.
_____

I replace negative habits with new habits that work for me.
_____

I let go of any harmful and negative habits.
_____

I have the power to choose and create new habits.
_____

Forming good habits allows me more time
to focus on what really matters.
_____

everyday
simplicity

declutter

Clean, open spaces give
your body and mind room
to breathe. You might
not realise it but your
physical surroundings
can significantly affect
your attitude and your
experience of happiness.
If you have a clean, organised
and bright space you are
likely to be more productive,
have more energy and
have more resources to
overcome any challenges
as they arise.

Calm confidence comes from a place where you can control your environment. There is so much in the world we cannot control and this can cause stress and exhaustion, but your own spaces are up to you. The art of clutter-free living is a life skill that, once developed, will keep you tracking towards your visions and goals, and enable your life to flourish. This is a simple promise you can make to yourself, for yourself.

Your space says a lot about you and your state of confidence, but the good news is it can easily be changed. Do your surroundings reflect the essence of who you are? How does your space make you feel? What have you been tolerating for too long? What are you holding on to, and what for? Is it inspiring?

Clutter is stuck energy; it is a gradual build-up of things, some precious, some not. Our spaces can end up holding so much that, before we know it, we are in clutter mode and we start feeling drained without really knowing why, as clutter affects us on a subconscious level.

Clutter creates stress. Ever found yourself walking in the front door to see piles of paper, school bags, lunch boxes, random hair clips, school notices, mobile devices and car keys on the kitchen

> Your space says a lot about you and your state of confidence, but the good news is it can easily be changed.

bench? How did that happen? Defeat! You just had it all cleaned up. Or you've opened your wardrobe and don't know what to wear because you can't really see anything as there is too much in it? Gone to sit at your desk and can't find what you are looking for, or you've missed a bill or credit card payment date because it was lost somewhere in the rubble? Life happens, and we are all busy doing what we do. However, when we are committed to living with minimal clutter and regularly attend to it, we live a much calmer and more confident life.

Essentialism by Greg McKeown is one of our favourite books. McKeown describes his philosophy as 'the disciplined pursuit of less'. With everything you do, buy, own and surround yourself with in life, ask yourself, 'Is it essential?' This one question allows you to quickly make assessments as to what you are doing with your time – and it also really helps when shopping!

'A place for everything and everything in its place.'

---

charles augustus goodrich

effects
of clutter

You lose things.

You waste a lot of time moving things
from pile to pile and searching
for what you need.

You spend more money buying
things you already have.

You buy more storage, but still feel out of control.

You feel overwhelmed by having
too much to do.

You cannot prioritise efficiently
and you get distracted easily.

people often have excuses – they are sentimental, they have young children, they don't know where to start, it is too overwhelming, or they are too busy to declutter. However, the reward of taking some time to work on this area is a feeling of freedom, calm, control and confidence; we become relaxed, organised and happier.

When you clean out your wardrobe – I mean empty it fully – and only put back what you use, love and enjoy wearing, the reward far outweighs the effort. You'll feel lighter, happier, more comfortable and so proud of yourself you'll want to tell everyone. The same thing happens when you tidy up your desk, clean it and make it an inspiring space; you can actually work well there and want to be there, you'll feel inspired to really work.

When we dedicate some time to this activity, it gives us back ownership of the things in life we actually can control: our environments, finances and diaries. Simplifying life is a constant cycle of balance, boundaries and gently testing those boundaries until you arrive at a place you're comfortable with. Start gently and you will gain momentum and become great at this life skill. It is such a joyous, confidence-boosting activity that will give you more time to be joyful, allow you to feel at peace in your own spaces and ultimately spend less time cleaning up.

Clean, open and inspiring spaces that are clutter-free give your body and mind room to breathe. If you live in a happy, calm and confident space, you will bring a new level of self-belief into your life. It really is that simple. Just start with one drawer and see what happens!

how to

decluttering task option 1

The best way to think about decluttering is to write a simple list so you don't feel overwhelmed.

decide

- Which space? Choose one area at a time.
- Revamp or overhaul? Small tidy-up or complete overhaul?
- When will I do it? Schedule it in like an appointment.
- Do I need help? Consider whether you need a friend to help.

define

- **Small steps** Break down the task into small steps so you don't get overwhelmed. For example all of the following should be approached as a single complete job in itself: pay bills; sort kitchen cutlery drawer; tidy make-up bag; clean out car; donate old magazines, books and trinkets; clean a shelf in the shed; go through all mail; sort old cookbooks; tidy the fridge, medicine cupboard or bathroom cupboard.
- **Full room** If you have a whole day to spare, choose one room, office space or area. For example: car overhaul, office revamp, clothing cleanout, lounge room.

do

- Choose a time in your diary that you can allocate to do the job. For example, make Saturday morning 10 a.m. to noon decluttering time each week, or take a full day to overhaul something each month.

decluttering task option 2

If the above method doesn't work for you, try the quick list below for a guide as you consider whether to keep or throw out each item:

- **Examine** What does it mean to me? What is the purpose of it?
- **Evaluate** Is it essential? Can I let go of it? Is it just clutter? Does it work? Will I use it? Do I care about it? Who am I keeping it for? Where will it go?
- **Eliminate** File, throw or donate it.
- **Enhance** Make your space work for you; make it soul-nourishing, clean, inviting and motivating. Make sure you can find whatever you need in minutes because you have clearly stored it, labelled it or given it some space.

acknowledge the feeling

How do you feel now? Free, confident, calm, spacious, off the treadmill of life? Most people experience this to some degree once they have done some decluttering. Now you can allow yourself to breathe, think and feel with a lovely level of self-esteem and confidence as you have just practised a healthy level of self-care.

Finally, prevent the clutter from coming back by making a habit of decluttering all the time. Justify your next purchase and try the 'one in, one out rule' (that is, whenever you buy something, get rid of something else), put things back in their own space and set time aside each night to do a quick sweep and put things away. You then give yourself a wonderful start to each day.

It's important to accept the fact that some things cannot be changed; if we don't accept this, it adds to our stress and anxiety. If you have young kids, there will be toys. If you have school-age kids, there will be papers, bags and homework. This type of clutter is part of life. Rather than battling it every day, do what you can to minimise the problem, keep it from getting out of hand and then let it go.

As well as the decluttering projects above we also have some daily commitments for foundational, clutter-free living:

When we are committed to living with minimal clutter, we live a calmer and more confident life.

- Use the one-touch policy – when you pick something up, put it away where it belongs, don't just move it. When you leave a room, leave it the way you want to see it when you walk back into it.
- Clean the kitchen after each meal.
- Place daily-use items (clothes, books, toys) back in their designated homes.
- Before you buy something, question if you really need and want it.
- Open mail each day.
- At the end of each day, prepare your space for the following day.
- Set up systems for incoming paperwork, bills, filing, and receipts, both paper and electronic.
- Create more natural light where you can: open the curtains and blinds, trim shrubs that block light.
- Bring nature inside with flowers and plants.
- Stay on top of your daily commitments with a clean, organised diary.

do you need to declutter?

personal environment	yes	no
Is your living space clean and inspiring?		
Is your wardrobe tidy and are all of your clothes clean, pressed and in good repair?		
Have you cleaned out all storage space and thrown away anything not used in two years?		
Do you have fresh air and comfort in your home?		
Are your garden and outside areas tidy and well presented?		
Are your appliances, furniture and equipment in good condition and not in need of replacing or repairing?		
Is your bed, pillow and bedding clean, comfortable and conducive to a good night's sleep?		
Is your car clean and in good repair?		
Does your home inspire you and give you energy?		
Do you schedule regular cleaning and home maintenance?		
Total your yes column = /10		

Three actions to complete this week

1. _____

2. _____

3. _____

chaos to calm

'The more
things you own,
the more
they own you.'

anon

what's draining you?

To help you identify the areas of life that need attention, simply tick the boxes on the drainers list that apply to you.

finances	yes	no
Do you have a budget?		
Do you pay your bills on time?		
Are all your financial records filed and in order?		
Do you save at least 10% of your income?		
Do you have a plan to clear old debts?		
Do you pay off your credit card debt in full monthly?		
Do you pay off other loans as quickly as possible?		
Are your insurances up to date?		
Do you have a current will?		
Do you have a financial plan for the next year?		
Total your yes column = /10		

Three actions to complete this week

1. _____

2. _____

3. _____

relationships	yes	no
Do you let the people you love know how important they are to you?		
Do you tidy any loose ends with your partner, parents, siblings and friends by having open, honest and authentic conversations with them?		
Have you let go of any relationships that drag you down or damage you?		
Do you avoid gossiping or talking about others?		
Are you in tune with your wants and needs and do you ask for them to be taken care of?		
Do you forgive people for past mistakes?		
Do you give your partner and family quality time?		
Do you empower your partner and children?		
Are you a person of your word; someone who people can count on?		
Do you quickly correct misunderstandings or miscommunications?		
Total your yes column = /10		

Three actions to complete this week

1. _____

2. _____

3. _____

wellbeing	yes	no
Does your diet provide you with energy?		
Do you avoid excess tea, coffee and alcohol?		
Do you avoid smoking and recreational drugs?		
Do you exercise for thirty minutes at least three times per week?		
Do you allow thirty minutes a day for relaxation?		
Do you get enough sleep at least five nights out of seven?		
Do you have a holiday at least once a year?		
Do you have a medical check-up annually?		
Do you have a dental check-up at least annually?		
Do you drink at least one litre of water each day?		
Total your yes column = /10		

Three actions to complete this week

1. _____

2. _____

3. _____

fun, creativity & the big picture	yes	no
Do you learn a new skill/activity at least annually?		
Do you invest in personal development?		
Do you laugh every day?		
Do you have a hobby?		
Do you express yourself in some way creatively?		
Do you seek out adventure in your life?		
Do you plan regular fun activities with your partner, family and friends?		
Do you participate in some form of community service/volunteer work?		
Do you have a one, five and ten year plan in place?		
Do you dream big and believe that nothing is impossible?		
Total your yes column = /10		

Three actions to complete this week

1. _____

2. _____

3. _____

What would it take to have the 'no' boxes you have ticked, unticked? What action steps would you need to put into place? What is most important to you on this list?

summary

- Stress is created by a cluttered environment.

- Decluttering leads to a calmer, more confident and happier existence.

- Simplifying and decluttering is an aspect of life that we can control.

- Decide what you are going to clean out and whether you need help; whether your chosen task is a small clean-out or a total overhaul.

- Put time in your diary to make it happen, then do it.

- Get in touch with the reward of feeling free, calm, confident and in control.

- Take time each night to do a quick clean-up and prepare for the following day.

- See what other areas in your life are cluttered and draining you and take some small actions to declutter them.

- Write a declutter list so you know what to do next, start with the end in mind.

- Get your desk ready to inspire and motivate you with no distractions.

power
thoughts

I live in a clean, clutter-free environment,
physically and emotionally.

Letting go of clutter helps me let go of stress.

I have everything I need.

My life is calm and organised.

Clearing my environment creates room
in which abundance can flow.

Clearing physical clutter helps me to clear emotional clutter.

Letting go of what is insignificant enables me
to fully enjoy what is most important.

Clearing clutter allows me to feel calm and in control.

People and relationships are more important
to me than possessions.

bliss
points

---

create joy and fun

The benefits of taking
time for yourself will
flow to everyone,
whether that's your boss,
your work colleagues,
your staff, your partner
or your children – and,
of course, yourself.

ind the joy! We are on a lifelong journey, so we need to find our bliss points and build them in for some lightness, laughter and joy. These activities fill our confidence tank and fire up our motivation, inspiration and energy levels, nourishing our souls. It's important to leave yourself space to include activities that you enjoy, that inspire and recharge you.

In today's world, taking time for yourself is often confused with being selfish, and we sometimes feel we have to justify ourselves to others when we do so. We might think of such time in negative terms, such as 'It's not productive', or 'I'm wasting time.' Often this attitude is something we've learned from our employers, teachers, parents and peer groups. It is hard to stop thinking this way, and to establish boundaries that may disappoint others. But it can be done; nourishing yourself is one of the best preventative medicines available to us.

Remembering that we are all different, our recipes for fun will be different. Some people gain joy by retreating into quiet – by being in nature or immersing themselves in a book. Others feel confident and energised by being part of a crowd, having a good belly laugh, hosting a dinner party or being physically active. Hobbies and leisure activites are important foundations to help us find purpose outside of just working.

When our happiness levels are low, our confidence is low, and the smallest tasks in the world seem like an overwhelming effort. Sometimes when you are tired, just making your bed seems to be an effort because you have been so dedicated to the work side of your life and forgot to nourish yourself along the way. The one person who can fix this is you, and it's vital to respect yourself enough to ensure you build this into your plan.

Think back to when you had some great fun, or found a deep sense of peace. Did you sit alone for a while in quiet, natural space, read a great book that you couldn't put down or sing in your car to the radio as loud as you could bear? The joy you gain from these times boosts your energy and confidence significantly and nourishes your whole being.

Don't put off hobbies, travel, learning, quiet time and fun until you 'have time'. There is never a perfect time to go on holiday, take a break or go for a walk, because you can always do more work and chores. Simply allowing yourself this life need is essential. You just need to do it!

Creating joy and fun is an essential life skill. Many of us were great at it when we were young and free of responsibility; we were able to let our creative juices flow. Then life and responsibility got in the way and it all became rather serious. Finding time for joy and happiness is critical to your wellbeing and overall health. So make the time in your diary. Put a fence around it and don't let anyone else take it. You have learnt the skills of planning, prioritising and execution; put what you have learnt into action and reap the benefits for yourself. What is the one thing you would love to do? What makes you happy? This is the week to do it. It doesn't matter if it takes five minutes or four hours. Make time in your schedule. Enjoy your me-time!

'Twenty years from now you will be more disappointed by the things you didn't do than by the ones you did do.'

mark twain

find
an area
of passion

Here is a list of some areas
of passion that you might like to pursue:

Travel	Nature
Fashion	Photography
Food	Books
TV & film	Education & learning
Music	Beauty
Interior design	People & connections
Politics	Cultures & groups
Socialising	Environment
Gardens	Social causes & volunteering
Fine art	

make a contract with yourself to have more fun and recreate some adventure and joy in your life. Most of our clients say that the reason they lack joy in life is that they are so dedicated to their work. We tell them that their boss didn't take their joy; they did. They decided to put work ahead of everything else important to them. Flick the switch on this one immediately. Once you put in the joy, your work flourishes along with a whole life outside of work.

What we find exciting today and tomorrow may change as we grow, evolve and become more confident in who we are. There are two main parts to the task here, which we describe in the following pages. Most people are not connected to themselves and what they are passionate about. These prompts might help you touch base again so you can create a lovely list for yourself to go out and have some fun, nourish yourself, and create joy in your life.

bliss points

what inspires you

Use this list to inspire you to get moving and book in some nourishing activities that will fill your happiness and confidence tank. The more of these we do, the more we believe in ourselves. Make the time, guilt-free, as these activities will bring out the best in you, enabling you to flourish and shine for those you care about most.

Explore somewhere new.

Be in nature.

Have a picnic.

Write in a journal.

Go on a date night
with your partner.

Cook something new.

Exercise with a friend.

Organise a monthly
catch-up with friends.

Give a compliment.

Book a holiday.

Ride your bike to work.

Try learning a new language.

Do something for a friend
without them asking you to.

Visit a museum.

Sit by a river and sketch.

Go to a musical or the theatre.

Get up early and
watch a sunrise.

Get to know some more people.

Go on a road trip with
a friend or your family.

Go for a swim.

Read a book.

Explore your own city
as if you were a tourist.

Go camping.

Learn a musical instrument.

Meditate.

Study and learn something.

how to have more fun

It should be clear by now that having time for yourself is not selfish, but self-care. That it will enhance not only your life but the lives of those close to you. To make sure you get that essential time, take the following steps:

1. Know what you want to do with your me-time.
2. Estimate how long it will take.
3. Allocate the time in your diary.
4. Take action to make it happen.

Putting it into your diary makes it real, and remember, these activities are essential tank-fillers to keep you balanced and nourished, and give you a strong sense of wellbeing.

summary

- Build bliss points into your life that will nourish your soul.

- Find out what you are passionate about to determine how you want to spend your me-time.

- Establish what you need to fill your fun tank and feel confident that you have a life outside of work.

- Choose an area of passion and then choose some activities to support it.

- Find something creative to do.

- There is never a perfect moment to take time out; you just have to do it.

- Have a good belly laugh every day.

power
thoughts

I have an abundance of joy in my life.

I make happiness the most important part of my day.

I clear my goals with cheerfulness and joy.

Every day my life becomes brighter as
I choose to think positive thoughts.

Being happy and calm helps me to realise my dreams.

My happiness is contagious among my family,
friends and colleagues.

I am a naturally calm and happy person.

I nurture my own positivity.

I laugh often.

I always make time to allow joy into my life.

14

glass
half-full

practise gratitude

When we take the time to
activate our awareness,
we experience a wealth
of things to be grateful
for every day. We can
then use these gratitude
experiences actively,
as a tool to create
a calm and confident life.

eeling an intense love for your partner, revelling in the fresh ocean mist on your skin, appreciating the intricacy of a beautiful flower, savouring a beautiful meal or a spectacular wine, or experiencing the sheer delight of watching your children play in the park are all forms of gratitude in action. You can also experience gratitude by acknowledging the help that someone has given you, or taking a moment to truly feel the success you have achieved. It is a sense of deep appreciation for what is in front of us. Connecting to the experience brings appreciation and, ultimately, gratitude.

When we find time in our day to connect and truly feel gratitude, we will instantly feel that we are incredibly lucky. Lucky to have simple pleasures that bring great joy and other rewards.

By slowing down and taking time for yourself during the day you are more likely to create new opportunities to infuse your gratitude practice. At the beginning it can be great to link your gratitude practice to something you already do; for example, every time you get into bed, think of three things you are grateful for before you go to sleep. Others find it more powerful to write their gratitude practice down, so if that appeals to you, getting a journal to allocate to your gratitude practice is worth the investment.

We see gratitude as a skill set that we learn and activate forever. When we practise gratitude consistently, it can eventually override the harsh inner critic many of us carry around with us, or our natural inclination to seek out the negative. Gratitude is a skill that the majority of people don't have naturally. In our materialistic society, we are often seduced into relying on the next handbag, next hot car, next big holiday, next new outfit, next next next . . . to make us feel invigorated. This is like getting on a shopping treadmill, running faster and accumulating more; this eventually makes us feel depleted rather than filled with happiness. That's not to say that a hot pair of Jimmy Choo heels won't bring a sense of temporary gratitude; sure it will, however, acquiring things will not create long-lasting gratitude. Instead, it is more worthwhile to focus on the things you might already have, such as your health, nature, the people around you, your next meal – everything you can see and feel where you are sitting right now.

Most people respond to this exercise by moving from a state where they never really feel gratitude to becoming gratitude detectives, continually looking for ways to experience gratitude because it feels so good. Gratitude takes us back to our core, back to our values, back to those qualities that we want to radiate like a shining light. Have you ever been around a person who is incredibly grateful and appreciative; these people are like magnets, leaving you thinking, 'I want some of what he/she has.' This feeling is totally accessible to each and every person on the planet. All it takes is the time to experience it and to fuel our tank of happiness. So often we can make our days so over-scheduled and 'busy' that we lose the opportunity to feel gratitude. This is about slowing down, working smarter not harder, and creating gaps in your day to put your gratitude glasses on.

Even if something you could otherwise view as negative happens, in what way could that be viewed with gratitude? For example, can you learn something from it? Did it challenge you to bring out some aspect of yourself that you value? Did it show you some aspect of yourself that you needed to be aware of and work on? Even in a space of feeling challenged we can train our brains to experience gratitude – that's once we have mastered the day-to-day gratitude!

Gratitude is also like a healthy dose of vitamins for our relationships. Often we spend a great deal of time looking first for the faults in ourselves, followed by the faults of those closest to us. Gratitude for the people closest to you, the things people have done for you, and the sheer joy they bring to your life, is the way to develop and deepen your connection firstly with yourself and then with the people around you. An attitude of gratitude is a sure way to supercharge the relationships and connections you already have.

There has been plenty of research around gratitude that shows it is the easiest and quickest way to fill your happiness tank. Research has shown that people who practise gratitude consistently experience a host of benefits, including higher levels of happiness, positivity, generosity and compassion.

These are fairly compelling reasons to make gratitude part of your daily routine, just like brushing your teeth. Building in a gratitude habit stands you in good stead for hardwiring happiness and feeling more joy.

Practising gratitude is like a healthy dose of vitamins for relationships. It will develop and deepen your connections with those around you.

everyday experiences to be grateful for

Meals   Meal times are a great time to put on your gratitude glasses. Be grateful for the effort that you or someone else put into preparing your food, grateful for the farmer who tended to the crop (if you've ever spent time on a farm, you will see the hard work that goes into getting a banana or an avocado on the table – the effort is enormous), grateful for your tastebuds and the experience of eating.

Transport   If you have a car, you can be grateful that it gets you from A to B; if your suburb is well serviced with public transport or good bike lanes, that is something to be grateful for. If you can afford to travel abroad, you can be grateful for the planes that so effortlessly transport us around the world; they are amazing.

Home   If you have modern appliances that make life easier, such as a dishwasher, fridge, and/or washing machine, be grateful for them; be grateful that you have access to pure clean water, and a kitchen where you can prepare beautiful meals. Or for your bed, which allowed you to rest all night.

Work   Be grateful for the role you have, the people you can collaborate with, the opportunities that exist, the bills you can pay, the talent you have.

Relationships   Be grateful for the love that you feel, the experiences you have shared, the connections you have created, the relationships you have nurtured; for the friends who support you and are there for you.

'Let us be grateful
to the people who
make us happy;
they are the
charming gardeners
who make our
souls blossom.'

---

marcel proust

how to

Developing your gratitude ritual will be like finding a shoe that fits –
one that is comfortable and natural for you. There are endless ways to
create more gratitude experiences; the most important part is to make
a start. Along the way you can find the best fit for you.

The most popular way is to journal your thoughts. Our simple routine is
to journal every night before we go to bed. We simply write down three
things we are grateful for in our gratitude journal. It is a powerful way to
express your dreams, desires, thoughts and feelings. Some nights this
can be just one word; other nights it might be five pages.

Many families also have a gratitude jar in their home. Each member can
write something they are grateful for on a little piece of paper each day.
Just looking at the jar filling up changes a down day into a good day.

If you would like a little prompting for your journal then this list of
questions below is sure to get the ink flowing:

- Who do I appreciate?
- How am I fortunate?
- What material possessions am I thankful for?
- What abilities do I have that I'm grateful for?
- What about my surroundings (home/neighbourhood/
  city) am I thankful for?
- What experiences have I had that I am grateful for?
- What happened today/yesterday/this week/this month/
  this year that I am grateful for?

- What opportunities do I have that I am thankful for?
- What have others in my life done that I am thankful for?
- What relationships am I thankful for?
- What am I taking for granted that, if I stop to think about it, I am grateful for?
- What is there about the challenges/difficulties I have experienced (or am currently experiencing) that I can be thankful for? (For example: What have I learned? How have I grown?)
- What is different today from how it was a year ago that I'm thankful for?

gratitude boot camp

If you are the type of person who takes challenges head-on and wants to immerse yourself in gratitude practice, then you may prefer a thirty-day gratitude challenge. This will prompt you to be grateful for something different every day. If this sounds good, the gratitude calendar on the next page is for you.

30 days of gratitude

1.
What is the moment you were most grateful for today?

2.
Which place are you most grateful for?

3.
What physical attribute are you most grateful for?

7.
What talent do you possess that you are grateful for?

8.
What is the title of the book you are most grateful for?

9.
What is the memory you are most grateful for?

13.
Who is the childhood friend you are most grateful for?

14.
What is the opportunity you're most grateful for?

15.
What personality trait do you possess that you are grateful for?

19.
What is the film that has brought you the most happiness?

20.
What is the music you are most grateful for at the moment?

21.
What aspect of your childhood are you most grateful for today?

25.
What has happened this year that you are grateful for?

26.
What success have you been grateful for most recently?

27.
What did you hear today that you are grateful for?

4.

Which family member
are you most grateful
for today?

5.

What did you do
today that made you
happy?

6.

What past challenge
do you feel thankful
for today?

10.

Which colleagues or
mentors do you feel
particularly grateful to?

11.

What moment this
week are you particularly
grateful for?

12.

What knowledge
do you feel thankful
for most often?

16.

What sight made
you feel grateful
today?

17.

Which friend
do you feel most
thankful for today?

18.

What act of kindness
are you grateful
for today?

22.

What happened today
that you feel
thankful for?

23.

What is it about
the place that you live
makes you most grateful?

24.

What new experience
have you been grateful
for lately?

28.

What new thing
did you learn
today?

29.

What did you
see today that you
are grateful for?

30.

What has happened
this month that you
are grateful for?

summary

- The fastest and easiest way to fill your
happiness tank is through gratitude.

- Gratitude is what makes the glass half-full.
It reminds you that you have enough and that you are enough.

- Gratitude is available and accessible to anyone at any time.

- Gratitude enhances relationships and connections.

- An attitude of gratitude helps to quieten our harsh inner critic.

- Writing in a gratitude journal is an outlet for expression.

- Starting a gratitude jar is a visual reminder that life is great.

- We have daily moments of gratitude available to us
if we slow down to catch them.

- Our next material purchase will only provide
a temporary gratitude hit; long-lasting gratitude
comes when we focus on what we already have.

power
thoughts

I finish each day with a moment of mindfulness.

The more I practise gratitude, the more grateful I become.

I prioritise gratitude as part of my daily routine.

I become more appreciative every day.

I am at my most calm when practising gratitude.

When I am grateful, good things will come my way.

I am deeply grateful for all that I have in life.

No matter what is happening in life, there is always
something to be grateful for.

I slow down and experience gratitude completely.

I am deeply grateful for all the positive relationships I have.

magnify
your
moments

---

master mindfulness

Mindfulness is paying
attention on purpose,
in the present moment,
and without judgement,
to the unfolding of
experience moment
to moment.

Often, despite all our good intentions and the work we do to regain control, we find ourselves getting caught on the treadmill again, losing confidence as the speed of life once again starts to get out of control. When this happens, it means that holes have been punctured in your tank and the fuel is leaking out faster than you can top it back up. The best remedy for this is to learn, experience and practise the confidence-boosting life skill of mindfulness.

Mindfulness means focusing on what is happening right now, rather than replaying things that happened in the past or worrying about what's going to happen next. Sounds simple, and it is. But that doesn't mean it's easy! It's really hard to stay focused on what's happening now, and not get caught up in the past or future. It takes a lot of practise to build the mindfulness habit.

Zen master Thich Nhat Hanh defines mindfulness as the energy of being aware and awake to the present. It is the continuous practice of touching life deeply in every moment. The practice leads to heightened concentration, which in turn leads to clarity and insight and allows us to be truly happy. Everything we do, from brushing our teeth, to driving our car, cooking, working and playing, when done mindfully with a relaxed attitude and open mind, can bring us joy and happiness so our tank is ready and full to handle challenges and the curve balls that life throws at us.

If we train ourselves to become more aware of the ordinary, life can very quickly become extraordinary.

Mindfulness can change the brain structure and improve our ability to focus. Harvard Medical School neuroscientist Sara Lazar's research showed that just eight weeks of mindfulness meditation can actually change the size of the key regions of our brain responsible for improving our ability to focus, strengthening our memory, making us more resilient under stress, fostering our decision-making, and helping us be more empathetic listeners and show more compassion to our colleagues.

why get into this life skill called mindfulness?

- It can improve focus, attention and memory.
- It increases your ability to feel happy and enjoy the good in life.
- It helps you identify your emotions, improving self-awareness and your ability to communicate with others.
- It can help to lower stress levels.
- It reduces your tendency to worry about things that happened in the past.
- It increases your understanding of your body.

'There are only
two ways to
live your life.
One is as though
nothing is a miracle.
The other is as
though everything
is a miracle.'

---

albert einstein

how to

---

start your mindfulness journey

---

breathe

The foundation of mindfulness and calm confidence is breathing. In our life we breathe, but we forget that we are breathing. Conscious breathing brings our attention to the in and the out breath. Our bodies are often in one place, our minds in another, and the one action that will bring alignment back is the breath. It is our faithful friend in any given situation. It will slow down and even park that Ferrari racing around in your brain. Mindfulness of the breath is about selecting some part of the breath cycle and paying attention to it as fully as possible.

There are many resources you can find to learn to breathe and there are many different practices that will help you expand your skills in this area. There are apps, breathing meditations, audio downloads and many books on the topic. But to simplify and just get started, sit still and follow your breath. Relax your belly as much as you can and practise abdominal breathing. Feel the air go in and go out. Sooner or later (usually sooner), your mind will wander away from the focus on the breath in the lower abdomen to thoughts, planning, daydreams – whatever. This is perfectly okay – it's simply what minds do. It is not a mistake or a failure. When you notice that your awareness is no longer on the breath, gently congratulate yourself – you have come back and are once more aware of your experience!

get in touch with your senses

Your senses are your gateway to the present moment. They offer us a great place to start and get confident with this life skill. They are available to us at any moment and they have the ability to transport us back into the present moment immediately. Remember that getting off-focus is a part of being human, and the more we practise these basics the more we appreciate our wonderful lives.

sight Look, acknowledge, see. Notice the view, the formation of clouds, the brilliant colours that are abundant in nature. Look at shape, light, texture and depth around us. Notice the flowers, the nature around us, the beauty. Drink in the view at all times.

hearing Close your eyes and listen to what is really happening around you. There are so many sounds to hear when you focus. In a café there are people talking, eating, there's music playing, coffee being made, orders being taken and the kitchen in full swing. There is so much to listen to and observe in close proximity but also in the distance. Wind in the trees, traffic in the background, children laughing. Don't judge what you are hearing, just allow yourself to hear it. Also listen to silence: it is powerful and re-energising, and you can hear yourself breathing. Silence is incredible, and gives us a great sense of space. Listen to what is being said, but also what is not being said, what is happening underneath a conversation; listen to someone's feelings.

smell Your sense of smell can change your hormone levels and promote calm. Luxurious lathered soap, just-baked bread, freshly ground coffee – all of these scents can alter your state of mind and reduce your stress levels. Notice the temperature of the air you are breathing in; identify scents; enjoy the smell of the ocean, freshly washed clothing, an open fire, a beautiful flower. Remember, don't judge, just allow yourself to acknowledge the smells.

taste Be present for all of your meals and savour every bite, such as the taste and cleanliness of a crisp apple, or a hot coffee reaching your belly and how it makes you feel. Notice what happens to the level of saliva in your mouth, notice whether something tastes strong or weak. Try not to only taste the first sip of your coffee, wine or juice. Focus on what the third and fourth sips taste like.

touch Skin, a soft blanket, a sandy beach, the different textures around us – when you are present for them and acknowledge them and how they make you feel, you can slow down time. Notice cold things, hot things, the feeling of a warm cuddle, a hot water bottle, a cool towel after exercise.

create your senses list to enrich your daily life

- Tasting a good cup of coffee.
- Splashing your face with warm water.
- Listening to children giggling.
- Relaxing as hot water from the shower hits your back.
- Smelling a delicious, rich meal in a slow cooker.
- Running your hands through your pet's fur.
- Breathing in the smell of freshly baked cakes or cookies.
- Admiring colourful flowers as they come into bloom.
- Putting on your old favourite jumper.
- Wrapping yourself in a soft blanket.

This is how we fill our confidence tank with the golden moments in life. They are around us every day, all day, and they are usually free. It is our distraction that robs us of the richness in life.

three other mindfulness practices to experience

take pauses

This is the simple practice of just taking a quick pause in what you are actually doing.

- Before opening emails, take a breath and pause before you log in.
- When you are rushing out the door with the children, just take a quick pause and look at them.
- Pause between bites of your lunch and dinner, and appreciate what you are doing.
- Before getting up, pause for a moment, take a breath and set an intention for the day.

walk mindfully

After a long day of sitting in an office, seated meditation might seem unappealing. On days when you want to get out into nature, try walking meditation instead. Walking meditation, also known as mindful walking, is an active practice that requires you to be consciously aware and moving in the environment rather than sitting down with your eyes closed. The practice brings you closer to nature and your body. It also helps strengthen your concentration, makes you more aware, and connects you to the present moment. Also, wherever you are during the day, walking around the office, into the school yard and around your home, instead of rushing, try to slow your pace down and be present with what you are actually doing. Your productivity and sense of deep inner wellbeing rises whenever you are aware of your body moving.

turn off autopilot

- Choose a regular daily activity such as tooth brushing, eating a meal, doing the dishes, washing, making your bed or going for a walk and practise the first two or three minutes of it mindfully, paying particular attention to the sensations involved.
- Do a couple of three-breath or three-minute mini-mindfulness exercises each day.
- Notice how you judge; observe your inner dialogue when you are in the mindful state and assist it with becoming kinder and more compassionate towards yourself.
- Look for opportunities to practise mindfulness, such as when you're in traffic or a supermarket queue, taking a shower, filling up your car with petrol – anything really.

As with all mindfulness activities, do not leave them too abruptly; always try to continue being mindful into the next activity.

List your five mindful practices to begin your journey:

1. _____

_____

2. _____

_____

3. _____

_____

4. _____

_____

5. _____

_____

summary

- You can start your mindfulness practice right now, doing anything at all.

- Breathing connects the mind and the body to become present and in the moment.

- Mindfulness practice fills our happiness and confidence levels.

- Mindfulness knowledge and daily practice will heighten concentration levels and strengthen memory.

- Studies show those who practise mindfulness regularly can physically change the areas of their brains that govern resilience and emotional control.

- The five senses quickly allow us to be in touch with the present moment.

- Mindfulness shows us the golden moments of life that are all around us.

- Mindfulness will allow you the opportunity to become more compassionate towards yourself and slow down your inner critic.

power thoughts

When I practise mindfulness I have a better
relationship with my loved ones.

I cultivate patience and understanding
through practising mindfulness.

Practising mindfulness enables me
to communicate with clarity and confidence.

When I take the time to meditate,
I become better at making decisions.

The more I develop my meditation skills,
the more in touch with my true self I become.

My meditation practice is my daily gift to myself.

I feel happier and more balanced after every meditation session.

I observe my thoughts without judgement of myself or others.

powerful
planning

---

make more time

When you get excited
about the skill of
time management you
will open the door to
more space, more sleep
and more time for yourself.
You will be much happier,
as you shift into the
driver's seat.

re you one to over-commit, over-schedule and overdo, all at the expense of your own health, wellbeing, happiness and confidence? So often we hear our clients talking about their time as if there was a time famine. As we are coming to the end of the book, hopefully you have spent some time on your vision, your goals, your habits and boundaries, as well as doing some decluttering, so now it is time to understand the important skill you will need to protect your space, time and wellbeing: planning like a pro.

Brian Tracy's book *Eat That Frog!* is a favourite of ours and it is all about time management. His number one rule for success is to think on paper. Once you write something down – a goal, a plan, a list, a dream – you stoke the fire of motivation; you own it and your inspiration to do it doubles.

We love planning, but many people don't. Our creative clients often resist at first, but once they have mastered this skill they find they have more time and energy and become more creative. If you think of success in the vegetable patch – how to grow a seedling, or a tomato plant that produces amazing, healthy tomatoes – it needs a structure. The right soil, plenty of sun, water, stakes, ties and so on.

We tell our clients to buy a week-to-a-page diary only. Our technology gurus often go back to using exclusively paper diaries where they can; however, if that's not possible they print out their digital diaries, a week

powerful planning

to a page. Having your diary on paper in front of you as a visual prompt is how you take ownership of what you are doing with your month, week and day, and you will be able to sort out what is essential versus what you don't need to be doing. Planning your time will decrease your stress, anxiety and feeling of lack of control, and let you steer your life where you want it to go. Remember, everything you put into your diary is your choice; if you don't plan your life, someone else will.

We have seventy-two blocks of twenty minutes per day. What are you doing with them to live your calm and confident life? One of the worst uses of time is to do something very well that need not be done at all. Putting pen to paper will help you prioritise and the result is a great feeling of freedom. A plan will allow you to go through life with a calm confidence and a great sense of overall wellbeing.

Remember if you fail to plan, you plan to fail. So before you start, remind yourself that clarity is key, know what is essential for you to feel confident, know your non-negotiables for your health and family, and beware of when you get distracted. You have your boundaries set up, so if you draw up your plan, stick to it and understand the rewards of a great life, this is one of the most joyous, creative activities you can do each and every day.

how to

---

become a master of time in six simple steps

---

1. create your year

A simple, quick and effective way to plan your year is to whip up a table of essential must-dos. This is a basic template that can be added to and updated each year. The basics are all planned out. Simple, effective, no thinking required. Just do it. Put aside a good hour. Start with your diary in front of you and book in for the whole year what is essential for you to feel in control, confident and organised. A good place to start is with the following:

- Your holidays.
- Public holidays.
- Weekends away.
- School holidays.
- Birthdays/anniversaries.
- Annual work commitments such as travel, conferences, trade shows and buying trips.
- Personal courses, such as meditation, business or hobby classes; trips, retreats and so on.

2. book in your non-negotiable list

Sample list:

- Weekly appointments with a trainer.
- Yoga each week.
- Monthly massage.
- Update finances on the first of each month.
- Haircuts.
- Dentist twice a year.
- Annual medical check-up.

Book in the things each year that are important to you; as if they are meetings with yourself and then, great – the base is done. Easy as that. Everything critical is booked in and you now don't have to think about it. We can always change it if need be, but 90 per cent of the time it doesn't change and you'll feel great about it, as it is all under control.

3. plan your month

Get out your week-per-view diary and have it in front of you. Go through the pages and think about what you want to do with your month. What is essential for you? The golden rule is to book in what you want to book in. Each time you write an entry, ask yourself, is this what I really want to be doing with my time? Eighty per cent of the time, the answer needs to be a resounding yes. Some things we need to do as we have responsibilities we can't avoid, but take control back as much as you can.

- Put in your essential monthly commitments to your work.
- Put in your kids' arrangements, sports, school and social commitments.
- Add your partner's commitments, travel or anything that you need to know that will affect your time.
- Put in time out – book in your own space, your time that is free and non-negotiable, a meeting with self.
- Add fun time: date nights, catch-ups with friends, hobby time, nature time, food preparation, exercise, writing and planning time.

Does the month excite you, or does it look over-scheduled? Do you need to cut back on something? Are you being your own time-robber by putting in too many things? We recommend putting rest time and couch nights in your diary because they are essential. And remember, it is okay to say no!

4. review your week

Each Sunday night, sit down and review the week you had and the week ahead. It will become second nature to sit on the couch and just look, ponder, refine and recreate the week to make each week as amazing as you can with what is in your control.

Look at the week ahead and ask yourself:

- Does this week work for me?
- Do I feel supported?
- Will it make me happy?
- Have I put in some special things for myself?
- Have I made the time to do what I want to be doing with my life?

5. own your day

The golden rule is to plan your day in advance. Before you leave the office, write a quick list of everything that's essential for you to do the next day. It takes all of 2–5 minutes, and it liberates you to know you are organised and ready.

Use your diary to put in what you will do and when you will do it. Prioritise in order of urgency and importance. To avoid procrastination, do the hardest thing first.

Most importantly, knowing that life does get in the way sometimes, understand what is non-negotiable each day to keep you feeling strong, calm and confident. Eighty per cent of the time, the only person robbing you of this is yourself.

'Give me six hours
to chop down
a tree and I will
spend the first four
sharpening the axe.'

—————————————

abraham lincoln

6. review, acknowledge, celebrate

When we do not pat ourselves on the back, acknowledge our efforts or tick things off with that pencil, it is hard to keep going, to stay motivated and inspired. Confidence needs feeding and when we see progress, ticks, things getting done, smiley faces, gold stars or whatever will keep us going, joy fills our tank. We fuel our sense of achievement, we feel good about ourselves, we feel satisfied.

It is a critical step that so many forget to take. Look in the mirror, be proud of what you did each day, be grateful that you invested the time in planning and owning your life. It is like taking a road trip – when you have planned how you want to get there, you will enjoy the journey. Without a plan, without knowing quite where you are going, it is frustrating, stressful and you end up missing all the sights on the way, because you expend all your energy trying to figure out where you are going.

Make that time for that precious person in your life: yourself. Give yourself the best chance to create the life you want by owning each day and how you are choosing to spend each precious block of twenty minutes. Surely one of those blocks can be for you to just sit still and enjoy.

fundamentals

you will require some discipline   Make time to plan. Once a month, go over your plan for the month ahead. Review your diary each day; treat it as a creative outlet. Every Sunday night, ensure your week is planned out for success and make sure it looks great for you. Put in the things that are critical for you.

you will need to prioritise   Ask yourself, 'What is the most important thing for me now in terms of health, family, finances and career?'

you will need to value precious time   Anything else you are doing, other than what is really important to you and what you have committed to, is a distraction. Once you have decided on your number one task, do it without distraction. Then you will discover how much time you have in the day.

summary

- You have seventy-two blocks of twenty minutes per day – what are you doing with them?

- Put pen to paper to really understand time, feel it and own it.

- Own your day – write up your to-do list the night before, work out what is non-negotiable and prioritise.

- Review your week – sharpen your pencil and really craft a week that brings you confidence.

- Plan your month – create space for yourself as you review your plans, and ask how you feel about them.

- Create your year – put in the most important things you know will happen.

- Take time to sit and plan, allow yourself to be clear, to prioritise and to understand what you want to do with your time.

- Review, acknowledge and celebrate. A vital part of feeling motivated, inspired and confident is to acknowledge your own achievements each and every day. It is an important part of understanding time and not wasting this precious gift we have.

power
thoughts

I have plenty of time for everything that is important to me.

I manage my time effectively and achieve what I need to each day.

Being organised gives me more time to do the things I enjoy.

I always have time for the things I love.

I make the best use of every minute in my day.

I am committed to managing my time effectively.

I decide when, where and how I spend my time.

I prioritise my daily tasks and activities.

I don't put off things that can be done right now.

I make the most of every moment in my life.

---

afterword

a few years ago we were about to present our first Masterclass of Wellness. We had a harebrained idea about bringing the skills you learn at a health retreat into the boardroom, as not everyone has the time or the desire to go to a health retreat. We felt people could still greatly benefit from our wellness 'tapas menu' of practical solutions for their own health and wellness if we came to them.

We have been life coaches for a very long time and live confidently with a strong base of wellness skills to support ourselves. We thought it would be fun to travel around and teach what we are passionate about.

We were nervous, scared, plagued with self-doubt and thoughts of whether we deserved to be there. Were we good enough? Would they like it? Would we speak well? And what would happen if they didn't like it? In the bathrooms we stopped, looked in the mirror, looked at each other and both said at the same time, 'Where are our power thoughts? Quick, let's turn things around and go in and share this great information.' We got a very quick hold on our thoughts, connected with why we were there and made it okay for ourselves not to be perfect, but still to have a go and share a message.

Now when we go on stage, we walk into jam-packed rooms of hundreds and hundreds of people, and without these skills behind us, we would practise self-sabotage like there's no tomorrow! Each and every single day, these skills are used to support ourselves and our clients, friends and family – and they work.

The clients we coach all say the same thing at the end, which is, 'Thank you. I now feel supported, I now feel that I have a simple toolbox; I can do a quick refuel when I need topping up, because I can just choose the skill I need to focus on to turn around the situation which is slowing me down or sabotaging my confidence.'

So remember that every person on the planet, no matter how confident their exterior is, how successful, how popular, will at same stage suffer crippling self-doubt. This is being human. But each and every day we have the opportunity to work with this, own it and keep moving in a forward direction; no matter what life shows us, the choice is yours.

Use this book to move through life day by day with enjoyment, self-belief and care, and motivation to experience your life with deep inner harmony.

May this book never be put on your shelf out of sight, but always be near you.

shannah and lyndall

chaos to calm

further reading

books:

Benson H and Klipper M, *The Relaxation Response*, Morrow, New York, 1975.

Duhigg C, *The Power of Habit: Why We Do What We Do in Life and Business*, Doubleday Canada, Toronto, 2012.

Dweck C, *Mindset: The New Psychology of Success*, Random House, New York, 2006.

Hay L, *You Can Heal Your Life*, Hay House, Carlsbad, 1984.

Huffington A, *Thrive: The Third Metric to Redefining Success and Creating a Happier Life*, New York Harmony, New York, 2014.

Kondo, M (translated by Hirano C), *The Life-Changing Magic of Tidying*, London Vermillon, London, 2014.

Lazar S, Hölzel B, Carmody J, Evans K, Hoge E, Dusek J, Morgan L and Pitman R, 'Stress reduction correlates with structural changes in the amygdala', *Social Cognitive and Affective Neuroscience*, Sept 23, 2009.

Linley A, *Average to A+: Realising Strengths in Yourself and Others*, CAPP Press, Coventry, 2008.

chaos to calm

McKeown G, *Essentialism: The Disciplined Pursuit of Less*, Crown Publishing Group, New York, 2014.

Nhat Hanh T, *The Moment is Perfect*, Shambhala Sun, 2008.

Peterson C and Seligman M, *Character Strengths and Virtues: A Handbook and Classification*, Oxford University Press, New York, 2004.

Rubino J, *The Self-Esteem Book*, Vision Works Publishing, New York, 2006.

Tracy B, *Eat That Frog!*, Berrett-Koehler Publishers, Oakland, 2007.

online resources:

Marano H, *Our Brain's Negative Bias: Why Our Brains Are More Highly Attuned to Negative News*, Psychology Today, 2003, available from psychologytoday.com/articles/200306/our-brains-negative-bias

National Institute of Health: National Center for Complementary and Integrative Health, *Relaxation Techniques for Health*, US Department of Health and Human Services, 2016, available from nccih.nih.gov/health/stress/relaxation.htm#hed3

VIA Survey: Find Your Pathway to Positive (The Only Free, Scientific Survey on Character Strengths), VIA Institute on Character, 2016, available from viacharacter.org/www/

chaos to calm

shannah kennedy

Shannah is a leading Australian business and life strategist and is the author of best-sellers *Simplify, Structure, Succeed* – the practical toolkit for modern life – and *The Life Plan* – simple strategies for a meaningful life. An Advanced Certified Life Coach and NLP practitioner, Shannah works with a diverse range of executives, business owners, entrepreneurs and sporting leaders around the world. She is a regular speaker and guest at conferences and offsite retreats, focusing on the importance of a life plan with simple strategies for success in life, both personally and professionally. Recent clients include Macquarie Bank, Deloitte, CBA, NAB, HPE, Mercedes Benz, Mortgage Choice, MTA Travel, Sussan Group, QBE and many more. Shannah's expertise has recently appeared in *The Age/Sydney Morning Herald*, *Business Day*, *BRW*, *Marie Claire*, *Herald Sun*, *Women's Health*, *Coach Magazine*, *Management Today*, *Australian Financial Review* and *Sunday Life*.

lyndall mitchell

Lyndall is a wellness entrepreneur, qualified and accredited coach, and founder of the Aurora Spa Group, Australia's pioneering, award-winning urban spa group. Lyndall brings to her work the 'hard yards' of running a thriving business; the knowledge gained from creating successful consumer brands, and the knowledge that comes from being a loving mother and spouse. Lyndall's professional background has led global corporate businesses, freelancers, business start-ups, busy mums and many people in between to achieve their vision of success. Lyndall is a regular contributor on wellness and lifestyle topics in the media. Recent coverage includes: *The Today Show*, *Australian Financial Review*, *The Age*, *The Sydney Morning Herald*, *Vogue*, *Women's Health*, *Body+Soul* and many global online platforms and publications. Lyndall has a powerful combination of hands-on business experience and more than two decades working one-on-one and in groups with busy, successful people who are feeling overworked, overwhelmed and overscheduled.

beyond the page

After reading *Chaos to Calm* you may ask, 'What's next?'

Shannah and Lyndall, The Essentialists, are internationally acclaimed educators of life and wellness skills. We will inspire, educate, support and guide you to make the changes you need to thrive personally and professionally. The best starting point after the book is firstly visiting theessentialists. com.au

We work with people and businesses from all over the world. Whether it's individuals, executives or entire organisations, we believe that with the right tools, motivation, guidance and support, we can all achieve our own vision of success. So whether you are interested in keynote presentations, workshops, career coaching, personal life coaching, or business consulting services, please get in touch with us.

We spend our days presenting around the globe to corporate companies, coaching, writing articles and books in between yoga, walking, and generally doing everything that we have talked about in our book, as well as, most importantly, raising our confident, resilient little people: Jack, Mia, Poppy and Grace.

It is an honour and a privilege to work with people that want to make change and is not something we ever take lightly. You have the tools and the knowledge to delve a little deeper and we are here on your side.

Keep it simple, keep it clear, and most of all, keep it all essential.

You can keep in touch with The Essentialists' community for frequent updates and inspiration. Follow us @The Essentialists on Facebook, Instagram and LinkedIn.

Your support of *Chaos to Calm* is truly valued and appreciated.

shannah and lyndall

theessentialists.com.au

chaos to calm

VIKING

UK | USA | Canada | Ireland | Australia
India | New Zealand | South Africa | China

Penguin Books is part of the Penguin Random House group of companies
whose addresses can be found at global.penguinrandomhouse.com.

Penguin
Random House
Australia

First published by Penguin Random House Australia Pty Ltd, 2017

10 9 8 7 6 5 4 3 2 1

Cover and text design by Adam Laszczuk © Penguin Random House Australia Pty Ltd
Author photographs: © Rachel Devine, reproduced with permission
Typeset in Harriet Text by Adam Laszczuk, Penguin Random House Australia Pty Ltd
Colour separation by Splitting Image Colour Studio, Clayton, Victoria
Printed in China by RR Donnelley Asia Printing Solutions Limited

National Library of Australia
Cataloguing-in-Publication data:

Kennedy, Shannah, author.
Chaos to calm : take control with confidence / Shannah Kennedy, Lyndall Mitchell.
9780670079483 (paperback)
Self-perception.
Confidence.
Lifestyles.
Self-help techniques.
Mental health.
Health.

158.1

penguin.com.au